Elisabeth Kübler-Ross is the author of

ON DEATH AND DYING

QUESTIONS AND ANSWERS
ON DEATH AND DYING

DEATH: THE FINAL STAGE OF GROWTH

TO LIVE UNTIL WE SAY GOOD-BYE

LIVING WITH DEATH AND DYING

WORKING IT THROUGH

ON CHILDREN AND DEATH

AIDS: THE ULTIMATE CHALLENGE

THE WHEEL OF LIFE

LIVING
WITH
DEATH
AND
DYING

HOW TO COMMUNICATE
WITH THE
TERMINALLY ILL

Elisabeth Kübler-Ross, M.D.

A TOUCHSTONE BOOK
Published by Simon & Schuster

TOUCHSTONE
Rockefeller Center
1230 Avenue of the Americas
New York, NY 10020

First Touchstone Edition 1997

TOUCHSTONE and colophon are registered trademarks of
Simon & Schuster Inc.

Designed by Jack Meserole

Manufactured in the United States of America

7   9   10   8   6

The Library of Congress has cataloged a previous edition as follows:

Kübler-Ross, Elisabeth.
Living with death and dying.

Reprint. Originally published: New York : Macmillan, 1981.
1. Terminal care.   2. Death—Psychological aspects.
3. Terminally ill children—Psychology.   I. Title.
[R726.8.K79   1984]   155.9'37   84-23686

ISBN 0-684-83936-9

CONTENTS

INTRODUCTION

Living with Death and Dying was written at the insistent request of patients, readers, and parents of dying children. These persons are familiar with my work and previous writings, but they have asked for more help in understanding the different languages terminally ill adults and children use when they try to convey their inner knowledge and needs.

We have presented most of this material in our teaching tapes, which are available to hospitals and teaching institutions. The material, however, was not easily accessible to private individuals and families who are more comfortable reading a book rather than listening to tapes.

So, here it is, modified and with added material from those who have had the experience on a very personal basis. May it add comfort and courage to those who are still afraid to talk about something as natural as the birth process itself.

Both birth and death involve great changes and adjustment, often inconveniences and pain, but also joy, reunion, and a new beginning. If it were not for our inner knowledge that we are on this earth plane for a relatively short time, then why should we strive for perfection, for love and peace, if it were not for the desire to leave this place a little bit better, a little bit more human than when we entered it?

We make progress in our society only if we stop cursing and complaining about its shortcomings and have the courage to do something about them. It is painful to admit our own fears, sense of guilt and shame, inadequacy, and low self-esteem; however, it is the brave one who admits these, the strong one who will fight his own negativity, and the trusting and faithful one who will see the light at the end of the tunnel.

I dedicate this book to the brave who have had the courage to fight negativity both within themselves and thus in our society.

ELISABETH KÜBLER-ROSS

Summer 1980

I

HOUSE CALLS AND HOSPITAL CALLS: THE CHALLENGE TO HEAR OUR PATIENTS

THE MATERIAL for this book comes from a decade of work with terminally ill adults and children whom we attended in hospitals, nursing homes, and, most important of all, in their own homes.

We have moved from institutional care of the dying to a new and healthier way of caring for them in their own environment; at home they are surrounded by their families and in control of their own needs and wishes, which is almost impossible to achieve in the best of hospitals.

Many of the readers will be familiar with my seminars on death and dying for health professionals in hospitals and the internationally held five-day workshops on life, death, and transition offered to professionals and lay people. These seminars and workshops have given physicians, clergy, counselors, nurses, and volunteers a tool to take back with them to facilitate their interactions with the critically and terminally ill. Our beginnings and lessons from the dying patients have been published in *On Death and Dying* and *Questions and Answers on Death and Dying.* For those who are not familiar with this material, the first chapters will repeat some of this material in order to present the remainder of the book in a more comprehensible fashion.

It is important to understand that the material herein is not really new. Yet there are millions of people who still have the illusion that a patient is "better off" if surrounded with an air of "all is well"; that is, if we visit terminally ill patients only with a smile on our face and cheerful, superficial conversation or silence. We have no problems getting them the very best in physical care and attention, but most often neglect their more painful emotional and spiritual turmoil.

Our work has included a total care of every need the dying may have. We have allowed them to be in control of the time and place of this care, of the amount of pain medication they require to allow them to remain conscious and alert, yet pain-free. We have respected their wishes to leave a hospital when there was no more active treatment available. We have helped in making arrangements to transport them home. We have always prepared the families for this change in their routine living and naturally spent time with the children who were affected by the sight, the smell (at times), and the communications and experiences of living in the same household with a dying parent, sibling, or other relative. We found it to be a profound and positive experience for most people, young and old—as long as our help and assistance was available and an occasional house call on my behalf alleviated the anxieties of the family.

Case Presentation of L.

L. was a thirteen-year-old girl whose big dream in life was to be a teacher. She was hospitalized during the summer and was found to have an abdominal tumor. After surgery the parents were reassured that everything malignant had been removed, and they were confident that their daughter's life was no longer in danger. Before school started L. developed new symptoms, and by September she began to deteriorate rapidly. It became clear that she was full of metastasis and that she would no longer be able to return to school. In spite of the pleas of her parents, her physician refused to put her on Brompton mixture for pain relief, and a search for a new physician who was willing to use this most effective oral pain management was in vain. She was no longer able to be transported to Chicago, where her previous treatment was given. It was at this point that I was consulted and started to see the young patient and her family in their home.

The mother, an open, deeply religious and courageous woman, spent much time with her daughter and discussed frankly all issues that her child brought up. L. was in a comfortable bed in the living room so that she was able to participate passively in the activities of her family. Her father, a quiet man, did not speak much about her illness or impending death but showed his love and affection in little extra attention and would often return from work with a bouquet of roses for his oldest daughter.

The siblings, ranging from six to ten, were brought together one day in the living room after school hours. I had a session with them in the absence of any adults. We used the spontaneous drawings of children, a technique taught by Susan Bach, and they happily cooperated and explained their pictures. Their drawings clearly indicated their knowledge of their sister's serious illness, and we discussed her impending death without euphemisms. It was the six-year-old who had the courage to bring up his problems, namely his inability to watch television, to bang doors, and to bring friends home after school. He felt intimidated by the adults, who started to tiptoe around the house, and wondered openly how long this ordeal might last. Together the children discussed the things they would like to share with their sister—all the things they would like to say to her prior to her death—and, needless to say, we encouraged them to do so without delay.

After several difficult days—each one expected to be the

last—L. simply lingered on. By now she had an enormously enlarged abdomen and her arms and legs were similar to the ones I had seen in the concentration camps. L. simply could not die. We brought her tapes of favorite music; her mother sat many hours at her bedside and was quite open to answer whatever questions her daughter had. It seemed impossible to figure out what held this little girl to life.

During one of my house calls—and with the mother's permission and in her presence—I asked her straightforwardly, "L., is there something that prevents you from letting go? You cannot die, and I cannot figure out what it is. Can you tell me?" With great relief L. confirmed this by saying, "Yes, I cannot die because I cannot go to heaven." I was shocked by this statement and asked her who in the world had told her this. She then related that she was told "many times by my priest and the visiting sisters" that "no one goes to heaven unless they loved God more than anyone else in the world." With her last physical strength, she leaned forward, put her fragile arms around my shoulders, and whispered apologetically, "You see, I love my mommy and daddy more than anyone else in the world."

My initial reaction was one of anger. Why do people who "represent God" use fear and guilt instead of representing Him as God of love and mercy? I also knew from past experiences that no one can help another person by demeaning another person's approach. This is the time when the use of parables or symbolic language is the only answer. The following dialogue took place:

"L., I will not get into a debate about who has the right answers about God. Let us talk about the things we always shared. Let us take your school as an example and answer me one single question. Sometimes your teacher gives especially tough assignments to some students in class. Does she give this to her worst students, to just anyone in her class, or to only very few, especially chosen ones?" L.'s face lit up and she said very proudly, "Oh, she gives this only to very few of us." My response to her: "Since God is also a teacher, do you think He has given you an easy assignment that He can give to just any child, or has He given you an especially difficult one?" A very moving, nonverbal communication took place at this time. She leaned up for a moment and took a long, hard look at her own emaciated body, her protruding abdomen, her skinny arms and legs, and with the most extraordinarily pleased look she stared at me and exclaimed, "I don't think He could give a tougher assignment to any child." It was no longer necessary for me to say, "And now what do you think He thinks of you?"

I made only one more house call. L. was at peace. She dozed off and on and listened to some of her favorite songs, including the one I brought for her from the Monks of the Weston Priory, "Wherever You Go," which has become one of the favorites of my patients. When she died, her family was prepared. The children came with me alone to the funeral home prior to the official visiting hours and they were most grateful that they were allowed to touch her body, ask questions, and say a last prayer for their beloved sister.

Death came early in their life, but it was a shared and moving experience to see a whole family growing closer together and sharing not only the pain and agony but also the joy, the music, the drawing, and the growth experience together. It happened at home, where everybody became a part of the experience and no one felt left out, as is the case when a child is removed from home and dies—so often alone—in a hospital, where children are not allowed to participate and are often left with guilt, sorrow, and many unanswered questions.

This case points out several issues that we have to be willing to face if we are to have the courage and conviction to be nonconformists and accept this fact: There are many people in the helping profession who are very reluctant to accept changes brought about by the new approach to dying patients.

There is no need to suffer incredible pain now that the Brompton mixture is available. There is no need to have a mother give around-the-clock injections for pain relief to her adolescent child, for whom this is painful and who is already reduced to "skin and bone."

Aside from the issue of pain relief, the next most important problem all of us have to face is the fact that each one of us is convinced of the benefit of our work. Otherwise we naturally could not spend 90 percent of our waking hours in this field. It is our belief, our faith and conviction, and, last but not least, the positive feedback of hundreds of families that affirm us. It would be easy to say, "This is *the* way to take care of dying patients."

In spite of the fact that we strongly believe in our approach, we have to keep in mind that we can never help another human being by discrediting another fellowman. As much as I am appalled by accounts and experiences of my patients and their families, it is a golden rule that we avoid, whenever possible, negative judgment of others even if we are in disagreement with their counsel.

The case of L. perhaps shows best how the use of the symbolic language, of speaking in parables, will help to answer the patient. It also demonstrates not getting involved in a form of power struggle and competition that can only bring about more hostility and negativity.

This is not to say that we should not take every opportunity to share with such an individual later and privately our positive experiences. Slowly but surely more people will see the benefit of this approach and gradually become familiar with it.

In the meantime we have to make every human effort to

8

teach not only adults but children, at a young age, that we can express our feelings openly and unashamedly, that there are people around who will express their opinion and understand them without the need to judge and label and discredit them.

If fears, like the one mentioned by L., can be elicited early in life and dealt with before a terminal illness strikes, we have found a way to preventive psychiatry. A group of six children, ranging in age from six to thirteen, have been confronted with their biggest fears and problems in a psychodrama setup, led by a small group of extremely well-trained adults who have worked with me in our life, death, and transition workshops. It was one of the most moving experiences that anyone who has been in the field of psychiatry and psychology for decades can witness.

It is most moving to see how children in a safe and accepting, nonjudgmental environment can open up and verbally express their deepest concerns. It is touching to see a nine-year-old finally find the courage to ask his mother, "Then why in the world did you bother to adopt me when you are so full of hate?" As a result of this openness, the other participants felt free enough to express their fears that they might not be loved or that maybe "my parents are not my real parents."

Our Growth and Healing Centers across the country, which are in a *status nascendi* at the time of this writing, will enable us to get to children of all ages and help them with these fears early in life.

B. is another case that could have ended in great guilt and tragedy if a friend had not intervened and assisted a young family to take the patient home and resolve the unfinished business virtually on the last day of her life.

I am using this example to show that children and adults have to be assisted in expressing their negative feelings and fears, resulting in a catharsis and an openness hardly ever possible during the restricting visiting hours in a hospital, where there is a lack of privacy and the ominous absence of young children.

Case Presentation of B.

B. was a young mother of two children, aged one and three years old. She had remarried when her little girl was two years old and expected a baby when her health began to fail. Shortly after the delivery of a little baby boy, she was diagnosed as having cancer and she spent much of her remaining life in and out of hospitals. Her young husband was not prepared to face all these new responsibilities: the care of two small children, the hospital bills, an empty house, dealing with neighbors and friends that he suddenly depended on, and most of all—he resented not having a wife and a "normal life." He had no one to confide in and held it all inside—until one day a few days prior to his wife's death, he lost his apparent composure and blurted out his dismay and anger at the world, God, and especially his wife. B., too weak to respond and unable to do much about her family situation, began to panic. She felt stuck in a hospital, where treatment had already been discontinued, where the bills mounted, where she was unable to see her children. She knew that her husband threatened to put her little ones up for adoption, and she was desperate to see to it that it was prevented. It was at this time that a girlfriend visited her, evaluating the situation appropriately and fortunately taking action immediately. After a consultation with B.'s physician, she was given permission to take her home. Friends contributed the necessary tools, from a hospital bed to a commode and a rubber ring. B.'s living room was converted into a sickroom. She was placed under the living-room window, where she was able to look out into the street and the garden. She was able to view the open kitchen and her children playing. Her husband was grateful to be spared returning to an empty house after work. A brief visit to their home revealed a very lonely man who never had any opportunity to share his own fears and feelings of loneliness and inadequacy. He was more than cooperative and quite willingly allowed me to sit with the little ones at the kitchen table, explaining death to them in a language that a three-year-old could understand. We drew cocoons and butterflies, and I told them that their mommy would soon die but that this was very much like a butterfly coming out of a cocoon.

We called her parents and sat in a circle around her bed. It was the little girl who broke the ice. Sitting on my lap in front of her mother, she asked three questions, each of them revealing how much this little girl really understood, each also allowing the adults to speak openly and frankly about their unfinished turmoil.

"Dr. Ross, do you think it is all right if I go to bed tonight and pray to God that He takes my mommy now?"

"Yes, you can ask Him anything you want."

"Do you think it is all right with Him if I then ask Him to send her back again to me?"

"Yes, you can ask that, as long as you understand that where Mommy goes the time is very different from here, and it may be quite a long time until you see her again."

"Well, as long as I know that I will see her again and that she is all right."

"That much I can promise you."

After a long look at her father and mother she said, "If this mommy dies now, do you think they will send me to a foster mother?" While the child looked questioningly at her father awaiting a response, the dying young mother looked at him, too. With a sigh of relief, he held his wife's hand and promised never to separate the children. The little girl was not so sure about this statement, when the mother looked lovingly at her husband and reassured him that it would be welcome and understandable that he should marry again and find some happiness (of which they had had very little in their short marriage) and also a mother for the two children. The little daughter then blurted out, "If all my new mommies should die, who would cook for me?" I reassured her that although this was most unlikely, I had a big kitchen at home and loved to cook. If this should ever happen, she would always be welcome at my house.

Shortly after this open and very loving interchange, the children fell asleep and we tucked them into bed. Their grandparents and the husband were alone with B. The candles were still burning and a soft John Denver song came from the tape recorder when B. made the transition we call death.

It took one house call, one friend who had the courage to initiate a move home for this young mother, and, as is often the case, the frankness of a little girl who asks questions and who gets answers instead of avoidance.

For the physician who can take an evening out of the usually busy schedule and to get to know the patients in their own home environment, it is an unforgettable experience and certainly enriches life in far more important ways than we can ever find in any other kind of service.

Children of dying young parents are a neglected group, since the critical illness of a spouse puts a tremendous burden on the other mate and leaves him or her little time to be of assistance to children. It is to the credit of a young and caring schoolteacher that this next referral was made, resulting in an unforgettable growth experience for all of us and for a class of primary-school children on the issue of death and dying—and the most beautiful example of preventive psychiatry in my opinion.

Case Presentation of D.

D. was a third-grader who had done well in school until the beginning of December, when her teacher noticed that she and her sister, a kindergartener, showed signs that something was wrong at home. They both looked sad, did not play with others in the playground, and became clinging and unwilling to go home after school. A phone call by the attentive teacher revealed that their mother was dying, that they had not seen their father in a while, and that no one had told the two youngsters the seriousness of their mother's illness. Their father left for work early in the morning, then visited his dying wife, only to return home late at night when the children were already asleep. An aunt, herself unable to communicate about this family crisis, took care of their physical needs. The teacher expressed her concern to the aunt and was asked to prepare the youngsters for the imminent death of their mother. It was at this time that Miss K. contacted me by phone in order to receive some guidance and assistance in this difficult task. I invited the teacher to come to my home after school to watch me prepare the children and to give her an opportunity to learn this approach so that she would be able to do it by herself in the future.

It was the middle of December. My fireplace was going, Coke and doughnuts were on the table, and we soon sat together—the four of us—in a cozy, comfortable kitchen, drawing spontaneous pictures, munching doughnuts, and chatting away. It was the third-grader who drew an enormous stick figure in the middle of her paper, with out-of-proportion red legs, many times the size of the rest of the figure. Next to it was a geometrical figure that she angrily crossed out before completing it. The following dialogue took place after completion of the drawing.

"D., who is this person?"

"My mommy."

"Anyone with big red, fat legs like this must have trouble walking."

"My mommy will never again walk with us in the park."

"Her legs are very sick."

At this point the teacher interfered with a correcting statement, saying, "No, Dr. R. Her mother is full of cancer. The legs are the only part of her body not affected."

"Right now, I don't want your reality," I answered. "I want to see what this child perceives." Directing my statement again to the child, I said, "Your mommy's legs look really huge."

She said for the second time, and quite convincingly, "Yes, my mommy will never again be able to walk with us in the park."

I then asked her about the strange figure next to her mommy, and she said with great sadness and some resentment in her voice, "This is a tipped-over table."

I repeated with a sense of incredulity, "A tipped-over table?"

"Yes, you see my mommy will also never again eat with us at the dinner table."

Hearing "never again" three times was enough for me to talk straightforwardly to this wise young child. I asked her if this meant that her mommy was so sick that she would die. D. said very matter-of-factly that this would happen very soon. And then—as happens so often—when I asked her what this meant to her, she said that her mommy would go to heaven but had no further answer. She had no real concept of heaven and insinuated—as so many of our children do—that this was an explanation grown-ups give, meaning that they should not ask any further questions.

I asked her if it would help her more if I would tell her a little about her mother's condition right now, since the children had been deprived of visiting her or of being informed about her in the last couple of weeks. I explained to her that their mother was already close to death, that she appeared as if asleep, unable to talk or move. I asked her to imagine a cocoon that really looked as if there was no life inside. We pictured a cocoon together, and I was just explaining that at the right time, every cocoon opens up and out of it comes . . . when she hollered, "A butterfly."

We talked for a while about how death was not the end, that the body that is buried or cremated was the shell, just as the cocoon was the "house for the butterfly," and that butterflies are much more beautiful and free. They fly away and we do not see them, but they then only begin to enjoy the flowers and the sunshine. Both children sat with open eyes, quite delighted about this possibility.

We told them that their mother's physician had promised to "smuggle them in" if they wanted to see their mother once more. They clearly understood that she could no longer talk to them or press their hands. We asked them to share whatever they wanted to tell her, even if she could not respond, that she could hear them and that it might also help their daddy, who was very lonely and sitting alone in the hospital.

All four of us went out into my garden and picked the very last mums. Then the teacher took it upon herself to bring the children to the hospital. She reported the next day, with tears of joy, that when she opened the door in the hospital, the children headed straight to their mother's bed, put the flowers on their mother's chest, and whispered, "Mommy, soon you are going to be as free as a butterfly." Father and children finally shared this moving moment, and the teacher left them alone, respecting the need for privacy among them.

The next morning D. asked to share her experience with her peers in "Show and Tell." She proudly went to the blackboard, drew the cocoon and the butterfly, and told her classmates, "Soon my mommy is going to die, and it is not really so sad when you think of a cocoon that looks like it's dead, but it only waits for the right moment to open up and out of it comes a butterfly." Her classmates not only listened attentively but began to share their own experiences with death in the family and death of pets. Before the teacher was aware of it, she had witnessed what was probably one of the first classes on death and dying, given by a third-grader to a most receptive and appreciative audience of grade-school children.

The most moving gratification came to my house a few weeks later in the form of a large manila envelope. It contained a letter from D.

"Dear Dr. Ross, I wanted to give you a consultation fee. I was thinking what you would like the most. I am sending you as a Christmas gift the letters and drawings of my classmates when they wrote to me after my mommy died. I hope you love it. Love, D."

Can anyone ever get a more moving "consultation fee" for a single hour spent with two delightful children, who were fortunate enough to have a caring teacher?

Both teacher and children have kept in touch with me. I receive an occasional letter or phone call from them. They have lost their mother at a young age, but they will not be traumatized by this experience. They have been able to share it, to understand it, and they in turn have opened up the formerly taboo topic to other youngsters.

To me, this is a form of preventive psychiatry. It is giving children an opportunity to deal with a problem openly and immediately, preferably before death occurs. It takes very little time. In each of the two last case presentations only one visit was necessary, one in the home of the patient, the other in my own home.

These interactions with patients of different ages and problems will perhaps give you a picture of our involvement and our joy in working in this field. It is essential that everyone caring for the dying and their families understands at all times their own concerns and anxieties in order to avoid a projection of

16

their own fears. It is equally important that we learn and teach the symbolic language many of our patients use when they are unable to cope with their turmoil and not yet ready to speak openly about death and dying. They will use the same "hidden" language when they are unsure of the response of their environment or when they elicit more fear and anxiety on the part of the helping staff or family member than they experience themselves.

They do need to express themselves, but they may not even be consciously aware of their deep anxiety to confront the truth. It is at moments like these that an experienced schoolteacher, a minister, or a counselor can use the tool of drawings, an expression of the symbolic nonverbal language.

Spontaneous drawings reveal the same information a dream will reveal. It can be obtained in a few moments in almost any environment—hospital, school, or home. It costs simply a piece of white paper and colored pencils. It sheds light within minutes on the preconscious knowledge of children and adults—a tool simple and inexpensive and easily accessible, as long as we have enough conscientious therapists who have been trained in the interpretation of this material.

A special chapter explaining the origin of this technique and its possible use for the dying and the living follows later in this book. It has been compiled by one of my students, whom we sent to England to study under the remarkable Susan Bach, a Jungian analyst, who specializes in the study of spontaneous drawing of terminally ill children. She has contributed more to the understanding of these youngsters than have many thanatologists who make headlines in an era when this work has become almost fashionable. She has worked quietly for decades in this field and has been most generous in teaching and training our own student, in order for him to return to the United States

17

to teach others the art and science of understanding the drawings, figures, and colors that these young patients use.

I think the most significant contribution these patients have made is in teaching us that patients do want to and can talk about their own finiteness, that they do know they are dying—and that includes hundreds of patients who have never been informed about the seriousness of their illness. Patients not only know that they are dying but can also convey to us *when* they are dying, if we are able to listen to them and if we learn to understand the language of dying patients. A small number of patients are able to talk in plain English about their own dying. Patients who can say, "My time comes very close now and it is all right," or pray to the Lord that "He take me soon"—those patients convey to us that they have at least partially come to grips with their own fear of death. Those are the patients that all of us will understand and they are also the patients who need our help the least. Patients who are "too young to die" will use what we call symbolic language. In order to understand the language of the dying patients, it is helpful to understand what the fear of death is. When I ask my audiences what they are afraid of when they think of their own dying, most people say that they are afraid of the unknown, they are afraid of separation, pain, suffering, unfinished business, leaving loved ones behind. This is only a very small part of the fear of death and not the significant part. Dr. George Wahl compares the fear of death with an iceberg. There is a small part above the water; the most significant part is hidden, invisible under the water. There are many things that we associate with the fear of death but they are repressed, unconscious; that is the part we have to understand. In terms of my own unconscious, it is very hard to conceive of my own death. I believe that it shall happen to thee and to thee, but not to me, like the psalmist who said ten thousand shall die on thy left and ten thousand on thy right, but it shall not happen to thee. If I am forced to conceive of my own death, I can only imagine myself being killed. I cannot conceive of my own death, except as somebody or something coming and destroying me. This is important to understand when you listen to patients with cancer. Even if the cancer has been diagnosed early, even if they have a chance of cure, they will always associate their malignancy with a catastrophic, destructive force bearing upon them. This is associated with a sense of impotence and hopelessness. If you comprehend this kind of definition for the time being, then you will understand the language that children especially use when they convey their awareness of their impending death. The symbolic language consists of two languages. Young children from the ages of about four to ten or twelve will use a symbolic nonverbal language. They will use drawings, pictures, teddy bears, dolls, or dollhouses—symbolic gestures to talk to you about their dying. Older children, adolescents, and adults employ more often a symbolic verbal language.

An example of the *nonverbal symbolic language* is that of the thirteen-year-old boy who was here at the children's hospital for over a year, waiting for a cadaver kidney. He was an angry, defiant, depressed little boy who was noticed to pretend-shoot little girls down on the wards, greatly upsetting the nurses who took care of him. One day I was asked to stop little Bobby's behavior becuase he had really become a problem in relation to the other sick children whom he threatened with his symbolic shooting. I went to observe him for a while, unseen by him, and I noticed he only shot little girls. So I walked to his room and said to him, "Bobby, could you pick on a little boy once in a while?" I tried to imply that I was not there to judge him for his "shooting and killing" other children, but that I was interested in why he chose certain "victims." He turned around and said, "Did you notice I not only pick little girls but they all have good kidneys?" I used denial at this moment, because I could not believe that this little boy knew more of the medical conditions of these hospitalized children than I did. I did not even know which of the children had kidney involvements and which did not. I went back to the charts of his "victims" only to discover that indeed he chose only little patients who had good, healthy kidneys. By his symbolic shooting of the little girls, he tried to convey that he was getting impatient and begging those children to die in a hurry so he would have the chance to live. I hope you understand that it is terribly important not to judge such patients! It is mandatory not to tell them that they are bad boys and that they should behave better. It is important that we understand the nonverbal communications of these desperate children and try to translate for them to help them express this verbally, so that we can share with them their impatience and anger—in Bobby's case in the face of his long hospitalization with so little hope for a kidney to come in time.

The symbolic verbal language is used by older children, adolescents, and young adults, but also by grown-up people who are simply afraid to die. But those are also the patients who are least understood, because in our nursing schools, medical schools, seminaries, and social-work schools, we do not teach the symbolic language sufficiently. An example of a symbolic verbal language is that of little Susan, who was in our hospital at age eight, dying of lupus. She was in an oxygen tent alone in a room, a quiet and good girl who never shared with other people her awareness of her impending death. Everybody liked her because she did not make the grown-ups uncomfortable, but she too knew about impending death. I hope that you remember the definition of the fear of death, that is, the fear of a catastrophic, destructive force bearing upon me and I can't do a thing about it. One night, in the middle of the night, Susan called her favorite nurse in and simply asked, "What's going to happen when I'm inside the oxygen tent and fire breaks out?" The nurse looked at her in surprise and said, "Don't worry, nobody smokes in here." The nurse then walked out of the room, but outside she listened for a moment for what we call the "gut reactions." She became aware that she must have missed something very important, but she did not know what it was.

This young nurse had the courage to listen to her intuition and called the nursing supervisor in the middle of the night. That takes courage, because most of us would have probably dismissed it and would have said, "Oh, it was probably not so important," because we do not like to inconvenience people in the middle of the night. She was fortunate enough to have an understanding, nonjudgmental nursing supervisor, who also knew the language of dying children very well. The older nurse told the younger nurse that this little girl was now ready to talk with her about dying. She advised her to go back to her room, simply sit down and listen to her. The young nurse did not feel comfortable doing that and again had the courage to admit it.

The older nurse came to the hospital, visited the little girl, and simply asked her, "What did you say about the oxygen tent and the fire?" The little girl repeated her question, and the nurse did something very beautiful: She opened the zipper of the oxygen tent, put the upper part of her body on the child's pillow very close to her, and said, "Do you think this would help?" The child started to cry. She thought for a while and then said in plain English, "I know I'm going to die very soon and just have to talk to somebody about it." They talked together for about forty-five minutes, shared all the things that had to be said, and both the patient and nurse felt very good about it. At the end, when everything was said that had to be said, the nurse did something that we do with almost all our new patients. She said again, "Is there anything else I can do for you?" The child gave a big sigh and she said, "Yes, if I could only talk once to my mother like this."

The nurse registered this request, said good night to the little girl, and the next morning took the mother into her office to share with her the dialogue of the night before. Everything went well until the last moment, when the nurse told the mother, "Then, at the very end, your girl said if she could only talk once like this with you." The mother suddenly got up, pushed the nurse away, and ran out of her office yelling, "No, no, no, I can't, I can't!" This mother never again visited her child alone. The child died without seeing her mother alone. The mother came to visit her at every visiting hour, but from that day on she always picked up three or four other children on the ward, in order to shield herself, to protect herself, so that her daughter would not dare to talk with her about dying. This was our mistake, and I'm trying to share not only our successes with you but also our mistakes, because I think you learn more from our mistakes 'than our successes. The problem we had with this patient is that we listened only to the child's needs. It is very important that we respect people's defenses. We listen to their needs and do not project our own needs.

In this case, we were very sensitive to the needs of the little girl, but in our ambitious striving to help this little patient, we became insensitive to the needs of the mother. If we had really listened carefully even to the child, we would have known that the mother was not ready for this kind of a sharing. Even the child knew it. She knew that her time was very close, that most likely she would die before the mother was ready to face it. When she sensed that her time was running out, she picked a substitute mother figure in a young nurse. If we had listened to this, we still would have invited the mother, we would have shared with her some of the communication, but we would have asked the mother to tell us when to stop, so that we would not go too fast too soon with someone who was not really ready to face things. We are not always successful, but it is important that we were honest with this patient, and told her that we would like to talk with her mother, but that we felt that the mother was not ready. We then became substitute mother figures, so that this girl could talk with a nurse about the things she would rather have talked about with the mother, if the mother had received enough help in time to face the death of her little girl.

I have spoken so far about patients' communications and needs to talk about their own impending death. I would like to say a few things on how patients talk with you when they try to communicate not the fact *that* they are dying but *when* they are dying. Sometimes I make rounds in the hospital, and I have an old European habit of shaking hands. A dying patient holds my hand differently, and I look at her and say, "Is this the last time?" The patient then nods her head. I then say good-bye to her and the next morning the bed is empty. It can be this kind of nonverbal communication that some patients use to convey that their end is very close. Another example is that of an old man who lived in our house. He was given two months to live—he lived two and a half years. We find it rather detrimental when patients are given a certain number of months to live, because the information is almost never correct. When this man was close to dying, I went to visit him one morning with a cup of coffee and a piece of cake. He suddenly looked up and said, "I want to give you a gift." I said, "A gift?" This wasn't like him. He said, "Yes, I would like you to keep my cane." It was on the tip of my tongue to say, "But you need your cane." The cane was his only important earthly possession; he couldn't even go to the bathroom without it. But then I listened to my gut reaction and I didn't say that. I accepted his cane and walked out of his room. When I went back to get the coffee cup, he was dead. I'm using this example to convey another important message to you, and that is that people do talk about not only the fact that they are going to die but also the timing of their death.

This is something that members of the helping profession can pick up from their patients, but it is almost impossible to pick this up when a member of your own family is involved. If this man had not become a member of my own family, after living with us for two and a half years, I would have been able to hear him. If this man had been a patient of mine, when he said, "I want you to keep my cane," I would have been able to hear it. I would have been able to sit down and say to him, "You don't need your cane anymore, do you?" and he would have said no and we could have talked about it. But his being a member of my own family, I was not able to hear it, and I was only aware of this communication after he was dead. I am saying this so that you do not feel bad reading the examples of my patients, thinking about the members of your own family who were dying and perhaps tried to convey things to you that you were not able to hear.

We have talked so far about the very end of life. Now I am going back to the beginning of the awareness of a terminal illness. We have asked patients if they would have been better off if they had been informed early about the seriousness of their illness, in order to give them more time to come to grips with it. The majority of our patients conveyed to us that they would have been better off if their primary physician had been honest with them at the very beginning, if they had been informed very early that they had a serious illness, and then had enough time to come to grips with it and ask for further details when they were ready to hear them. Patients who made this request, however, added two conditions, both of which have to be fulfilled for a patient to come to grips with his impending death.

The more important one is that the physician should always allow for hope. It is important to know that hope at the beginning of a serious illness is something totally different from the hope at the end of life. At the beginning of a malignancy, for example, a patient's hope is always that the diagnosis is not true. When the diagnosis is verified, that the malignancy is in an early stage and still treatable, the hope of this stage is always associated with cure, treatment, or prolongation of life. When those three are no longer probable—and I'm not saying possible, because there are always exceptions to the rule—then the patient's hope changes to something that is not associated with cure, treatment, or prolongation of life. The patient may simply say one day, "I hope my children are going to make it," or, "I hope God will accept me in His garden." This is hope, too.

The second condition is that the primary physician does not desert the patient. This simply means that we still care for him as a human being, when a patient's condition cannot gratify the physician's need to cure, to treat, to prolong life.

In order to teach what we learned from our dying patients, we began to look for common denominators, and we found that most of our patients go through five stages. At the beginning of the awareness of a potentially terminal illness, the first reaction is usually one of shock and denial. That is what we call the "no, not me" stage. Most people do not believe it can happen to them, that it will happen to thee and to thee, but not to me. When patients are in the stage of denial, they cannot hear what you are trying to convey to them. If the physician gives them details of their serious illness, they register them briefly and then repress them. Very often, back to work, they pretend that nothing serious has happened to them, put their head in the sand. Others may go from doctor to doctor, from hospital to hospital, in a desperate search for someone to tell them that it is not true. When a patient is in the stage of denial, there are two things you can do for him. The first thing is to double-check whether this is your problem or the patient's own need. Nine out of ten patients referred to us supposedly in the stage of denial are not really in the stage of denial, but they pick up very quickly that *you* cannot talk about it. This shows by the fact that you come into their room and talk about the beautiful flowers or the nice weather outside. They then play into this conspiracy of silence in order that you will not desert them. If you have double-checked and you are sure that this is not your denial, you can convey to these patients the idea that whenever they want to talk about it, you will be reachable. When a patient then drops his denial and can talk about it briefly with another human being, he will remember this remark and he will call you. Unfortunately, patients usually drop their denial not between 9:00 A.M. and 4:30 P.M., but in the middle of the ·night, most of them around 2:00 or 3:00 A.M. This is the time when they are waking up, when their defenses are down, when it is quiet, lonely, and dark in the room, and then it hits them—that's what it's going to be like! It's then they should be able to ring a bell, and the clergy, nurse, or friend should be able to tiptoe in the room, sit down, and simply say, "Do you feel like talking about it?" If you can do that, you can hear more in ten minutes at 3:00 A.M. than in ten hours during the daytime. That is when a patient can talk about his fears, his needs, his fantasies, his hopes, and his unfinished business, very often to resume his denial during the daytime with people who do not feel comfortable talking about these things. I will give you two examples: one of a woman who needed denial to the very end of her life; another of a man who appeared to be in a stage of denial but who obviously knew what was going on around him, although nobody else was comfortable facing this fact.

The first example is Mrs. W., a twenty-eight-year-old mother of three small preschool children. She had liver disease and because of her liver disease, she slipped in and out of hepatic coma, confusional states, and psychotic episodes. She was a young woman who felt that she was too young to die. She never really had the time to be with her children. During these times of confusion she was totally disoriented. She went in and out of the hospital; her husband took out a loan to pay for the hospital and doctor bills. He had babysitting problems, and he finally asked his own mother to come into the household and take care of the children. The mother-in-law did not tolerate the daughter-in-law well. She would have liked to get it over with as soon as possible.

The young father was in great distress because of his financial problems and the whole mixed-up state of the household. One day he came home from work tired and desperate, and he blurted out to his dying wife, "It would be better if you would live and function as a housewife and mother for one single day than drag out this misery any longer!" This young woman sensed that her husband counted the days; the mother-in-law wanted to get it over with as soon as possible; the three children did not make it any easier, but they made her feel even more guilty for dying on them. In her desperation, she went to the hospital in search of hope. A young resident who was busy that day told her simply, "There is nothing else I can do for you." He dismissed her without giving her another clinic appointment.

What would you do if you were this young woman? She had three defenses available. For a brief period she felt a homicidal rage. Then she contemplated suicide for a while—but she really didn't want to die. It is most likely that such patients then develop a delusion of living in a more merciful world, and this is true of people who ordinarily do not use a psychotic defense. This woman did not need any of these three defenses at the time. She had a neighbor who was able to listen to her and who told her, "Don't you ever give up hope. If nobody and nothing gives you hope, you can always go to a tabernacle!" The neighbor took her to the priest in the hope that he could hear her.

But he could not hear this woman because of his own needs. He told her that a good Catholic does not go to a tabernacle. What he did not hear is that this patient did not ask for a faith healer, but basically asked for hope, which he would have naturally been able to give her. She left the priest more distraught, more upset, even in doubt about her own religious faith. She did go to the faith healer anyway, and she left the tabernacle supposedly cured and healed. And then she did something that turns a lot of people off—she walked around telling everyone about God's miracle, how God had cured and healed her. People avoided her. She was found a few days later in her home, not taking her medication, not sticking to the diet she desperately needed. She lapsed again into hepatic coma and she was dropped in the emergency room by her family, who could not tolerate the situation anymore. They didn't even want to wait for the physician to come.

On the medical ward, the same tragedy. The patient was well taken care of as long as she was critically ill, but as soon as she was out of her hepatic coma, she became a disliked patient. She did not behave as one ought to behave. Instead of being grateful that they had pulled her out of a hepatic coma once more, she walked up and down the hallway in a flowing nightgown telling everyone about God's miracle and how God had cured and healed her. The medical floor did not want to keep this patient and requested a transfer to the psychiatric floor. The psychiatric floor did not like terminally ill patients and they did not want her either. We call this the Ping-Pong game. The Ping-Pong game is a tragic occurrence in our large teaching hospitals. And although these discussions are done behind closed doors, the patient senses very quickly that nobody wants him.

When I saw this woman in consultation, I was very impressed that she could talk only about God's miracle. She couldn't even talk about her own children. I talked with her about God's miracle, but while listening to her I also looked at the night table and at all the things that she surrounded herself with. I was impressed that this woman had brought along all the things that a woman would take along when she goes to a motel for a few weeks. The hair curlers, books, and writing papers obviously implied that she knew that she was going to stay in the hospital for a long time. Then it dawned on me that this was one of those patients who needed denial probably until the end of her life because the reality of her situation was much too difficult to bear. I did something that we do very rarely in psychiatry. I told her that I would help her to maintain her denial, that I would never talk with her about the seriousness of her illness or about her dying, under two conditions. One was that she would allow us to help her, which implied that she had to stick to her diet and take her medication. The second one was that she would stop going to the cafeteria to stuff herself, which was a disguised suicide attempt. I did not tell her that she could not float up and down the hallways anymore talking about God's miracle, but it was impressive that this woman stopped this behavior the moment she knew that somebody would visit her often and would not desert her.

I went to see this woman at every moment possible. I think she taught me the meaning of unconditional love. She was the loneliest patient I have ever seen in all my years as a physician. She was kept on the medical floor, but she was put in the last room at the end of the hallway, the farthest from the nursing station. Not one door closed, but two doors closed forever. She never had a visitor. She was the picture of utter loneliness and isolation. One day I visited her and looked at her, restlessly sitting at the edge of the bed, with disheveled hair, with the telephone off the hook but she not talking into it. I said, "What in the world are you doing?" She looked at me with a pitiful smile and said, "Oh, just to hear a sound." This is the loneliness of the dying patients that I am referring to. A few weeks later when

I continued to visit her, I was shocked by the smell and the stuffiness of her room. My gut reaction was to open the windows and let some fresh air into the room. When I took a second look at her, lying in her bed, stiff, with her arms down at the sides of her body and a peculiar smile on her face (a psychiatrist would call that a hebephrenic smile), I blurted out, "What in the world are you smiling about?" The implication was, God—there isn't a thing in this room that could make me smile! She looked at me almost surprised and said, "Don't you see those gorgeous mimosas, those beautiful flowers that my husband has surrounded me with?"

Do you understand what this patient was talking about? Needless to say, there were no flowers in the room. We had regarded this woman as psychotic, which means poor reality testing. On some level she had excellent reality testing. She knew very well that she could not continue to live without some expressions of love forthcoming, preferably from her husband; but she was realistic enough to face the fact that these expressions of love, or flowers, would not be forthcoming until after her death, when she was in her casket. So, in order to live, she had developed an illusion sent to her by her husband after her death.

What would you do if you were to visit this patient and understand this symbolic language? Would you help her face the reality and open the windows and "get some fresh air in here"? Or would you refer to the flowers, which you know she had to see in order to live, even if you could not see any flowers? To open the windows and get some fresh air into the room would be tactless honesty, which does not help. I am sure many of you would be tempted to refer to the flowers because you knew that she had to see these flowers in order to live; but you don't need to do that! If you do not see the flowers, you should never pretend that they are there. I was very tempted to go home to my own garden and pick some real flowers and bring these to her, but this also was not necessary. What did this patient really ask for? Did she ask for flowers? No! This patient simply asked for some love, again, preferably from her husband. We were not able to get her husband reinvolved. This is the most difficult part of working with dying patients and their families. When a family has switched gears and has "written a patient off," it is impossible to get them reinvolved. This is where we come in as a substitute love object or family.

I simply sat with her. I did not open the windows, I did not bring her any flowers. I simply sat with her, holding her hand, being with her. One of my last visits with her, I sat there obviously wanting to talk about it badly. I looked at her with some questioning in my eyes, implying, Is it all right if we finally talk about it? She smiled and said, "You know, I hope when my hands get colder and colder, I hope I have warm hands like yours holding mine." Does this woman talk about dying? If you accept this kind of communication as also talking about dying, which we obviously do, then I must say that all of our thousands of patients have talked about their dying, whether they remained in a stage of denial or were able to proceed through the next stages. Among all the many patients we have followed, only very few needed to stay in the stage of denial until the very end. It is very important that you do not tear down this denial, that you respect the patient's needs and the patient's defenses. But even those who maintained denial to the very end were able to talk about the awareness of their impending death in symbolic verbal and nonverbal language.

My second example is a fifty-three-year-old man, Mr. H., who was hospitalized with metastatic carcinoma. He was beyond medical help, and his disposition became a problem because his wife refused to take him home to die. She was very disappointed in her husband, who had apparently never gratified her needs. She had two basic needs or dreams that were never met. Her big dreams had always been to have a man with big strong muscles, and a man who brought a lot of money home; he never met either need. She was resentful and bitter when he became "nothing but skin and bones" and the bills piled up, and she decided that she would send him to a nursing home to die rather than to take him home for his final care. In this way, she would be able to pursue her work and make money and she would not be "bothered" by him. The problem became an imminent one when the nursing home had a bed available for the next day, but Mr. H. had not been informed yet about the impending hospital discharge and transfer to the nursing home. The physicians did not know quite how to tell a fifty-three-year-old man that he had to go and die in a nursing home. The nurses who always complain about the physicians, that they are not honest with their patients, were given the okay to proceed telling Mr. H. Their response was that this was not their job, it was a social worker's job! A social worker finally visited Mr. H. with all good intentions of telling him that he had to go to a nursing home. But she soon became aware that his next question would be, "Why can't I go home?" and she would then be forced to tell him that his wife did not want him home and that he had cancer. The social worker finally called me in for help and consultation.

When I went to see Mr. H., I told him that I had a seminar in which we tried to learn to communicate with very sick and dying patients. He very quickly agreed to come to the seminar, and on the way to the classroom I asked him why he had said yes, when everyone predicted that he would not agree to come. He said, "Oh, this is very simple. It is because you used the word 'communication.' I tried so desperately to communicate with my wife, but I just can't seem to do it, and now I have so little time left." In one statement Mr. H. had told me about his unfinished business and also about his awareness that he had very little time left. In the classroom I asked him, "Mr. H., how sick are you?" He said, "Do you really want to know?" I said, "Yes!" and meant it. And he said, "I'm full of cancer." My initial reaction was one of fear and almost anger; I thought that this man had fooled everybody. Physicians, the nurses, the social worker, and his own wife believed that he could not take the bad news, and here this man knew all along. My fear concerned how to tell him that he had to go to the nursing home the next day. At this moment, he looked up, almost like a mischievous boy, and said, "You know, Dr. Ross, not only do I know that I am full of cancer, I also know that I have to go to a nursing home." I asked him how he knew all this, and he said with a bigger smile on his face, "You wouldn't be married to my wife for twenty-five years without knowing her." We asked Mr. H. then how we could help him, and he became immensely sad and said, "You can't help me . . . nobody can really help me except my wife, but she won't do it. I have never gratified her needs and, when I listen to her, it's like I could die tomorrow and there was nothing that had meaning and value and purpose in my life. It is very sad to die this way." It is obvious that he needed to hear from his wife that there was something in his life that was purposeful, and she was not about to convey this to him. I told him that I would like to talk to his wife prior to his leaving the hospital the next morning, and he laughed in my face and said, "You don't know my wife. She is three hundred pounds of anger and she would never come and talk to a head-shrinker."

I tried anyway. After this interview, which left this patient with so much unfinished business, I had to try to convey to his wife how important it was that she communicate something positive about this man's life. I called her and asked her if she would come in the next morning, before taking him to the nursing home, so I could talk with her for a half hour. She agreed to come, reluctant and angry as her husband had described her. She sat behind my desk and repeated almost verbatim what Mr.

H. told us she felt about him. She said that her husband was weak, that he never gratified her needs, that he never brought much money home and was so weak in fact that one day she gave him a lawn mower and he fainted. She continued with the most derogatory statements about her own husband until I had had enough and asked her to stop. I repeated some of her derogatory statements to her and told her that I was doing this in order to be sure that I had heard her right. I went on, saying, "What you are really saying about your husband is that he was weak and that he could die tomorrow and nobody would even know that he had lived. He was so weak that one day you gave him a lawn mower and he fainted."

In the midst of my repeating her own statements to her, she suddenly got up, furious, yelling at me, "How dare you talk to me like this about my husband!" My gut reaction was to duck, because I thought she was going to hit me over the head, when in the same breath, in the same sentence, she added, "He was the most honest and most loyal man that has ever lived!" My reaction changed very quickly to one of great admiration that she was able to say the two things that her husband needed to hear so desperately. I then told her why I had done what I did and asked her if she ever said these good things to her husband. She said, "You don't say those things to your husband." To me this is like never telling anybody "I love you" and then coming up with these schmaltzy eulogies at the end of their life. I tried to tell her that it was important that she convey these feelings to him, but I was not sure that she was able to hear it.

I asked for her permission to say good-bye to him, when she was on her way to taking him to the nursing home. We went together to his room and in the doorway she became angry once more, yelling at him, "I told this woman that you were the most honest and most loyal man that has ever lived." The big smile on his face conveyed to me that he knew he had finished his unfinished business. I said good-bye to him, and Mrs. H. took him to the nursing home, where he died a few weeks later in peace and acceptance.

This is an example of a man everybody was convinced was in a stage of denial. It is very important when you are not sure that you ask an honest, straightforward question. The patient will tell you how much he knows. If you have patients in this kind of pseudodenial, it takes one person to be honest and open with the patient, and the patient will then share the fact that he has known all along. In this case, our role was merely that of a catalyst, and this is probably the role that we have to play in nine out of ten cases. Very few patients need ongoing psychotherapeutic encounters. Most of the time, our role requires little time. We have to elicit the patient's needs, hopes, and unfinished business, and then we have to find out who is able to gratify those last needs.

When a patient has one human being with whom he can talk openly, he is then able to drop his stage of denial and go on to the second stage, the stage of rage and anger. That is the stage that we call the "why me?" stage. Those are the patients who are nasty, ungrateful, critical, and make life difficult for anybody around them. When an intern walks into the patient's room, he is greeted with the statement "Did you ever hit the vein the first time?" When a nurse comes in with a pain medication, she is greeted with the nasty remark: "You are ten minutes late. You don't care if I suffer. You probably have to have a coffee break first." When family members and relatives come and visit, they are criticized for coming either too early or too late.

What is your gut reaction to these nasty, critical patients? We either kill them with kindness, which is the worst kind of hostility, or we control our anger, but let it out on the student nurses. If we don't have student nurses, we let it out on our husband when he comes home, and if we don't have a husband, we kick the dog. Somebody always gets it, and to me this is very tragic, because we should teach our students that this anger is a blessing and not a curse. Again, we have to try not to judge those patients, but try to understand what they are really so angry about. They are often really not angry at you, but more often at what you represent. If you come in the picture of life, health, pep, energy, and functioning, you rub their faces in what they are in the process of losing. What the patient basically says is, "Why is this happening to me? Why can't this happen to you, or to you?" The peppier, the more energetic you come in, the more likely you get the patient's rage, envy, and anger. I give you a brief clinical example of anger:

We had a twenty-one-year-old man with lymphosarcoma who was hospitalized and in protective isolation for six weeks. He was totally isolated by the staff, who were very uncomfortable with him. Anybody who walked into his room got a nasty look, and the patient would turn his back toward you and stare at the wall. The staff avoided him. He was the picture of loneliness and isolation.

When I was asked for a consultation, I tried to communicate verbally with him and he treated me the same way. He turned his back toward me and was unable to communicate. I tried every possible way to reach him, and finally I gave up and headed toward the door. The moment I had the doorknob in my hand, I realized I was doing exactly what I tell my students not to do—I was walking out on him. So I went back to his bedside, and because he didn't communicate verbally with me, I was forced to look at the wall that this young man had faced for six weeks. I suddenly had an intense gut reaction of rage and anger. I looked at him and said, "Bob, doesn't that make you mad? You lie on your back in this room for six weeks staring at this wall covered with these pink, green, and blue get-well cards?"

He turned around abruptly, pouring out his rage, anger, envy, directly at all the people who could be outside enjoying the sunshine, going shopping, picking a fancy get-well-soon card, when they knew darn well he wasn't going to get well. And then he continued to talk about his mother, who "spends the night here on the couch. Big deal! Big sacrifice! Every morning when she leaves, she makes the same statements—'I better get home now, I have to take a shower!' " And he went on, looking at me, most full of hate, saying, "And you, too, Dr. Ross, you are no good! You, too, are going to walk out of here again."

Do you understand what these patients are angry about? They are angry with you for what you represent. You can go shopping, you can take a shower, you can go and have coffee. You rub in what the patients are in the process of losing. If you can help them ventilate this anger and rage and not judge them —you can help them sometimes in five minutes—they will not call the nursing station all the time and they will very often need one-half the amount of pain medication. You can truly help these patients say "Why me?" without the need to answer this question.

Families and staff go through the stage of anger, too. I visited a mother who stood outside of the room of her dying child. She looked like a pressure cooker ready to erupt. I asked her, "Do you feel like screaming?" She turned around and said, "Do you have screaming rooms in the hospital?" I said, "No, we have a chapel." Then she was able to pour out her sense of impotent rage. "Who needs a chapel? I want to scream and yell at God— 'Why do you let this happen to my child?' " I took her to my office, encouraging her to scream. Many simply try to cry on your shoulder, "Why is it happening to me, why is it happening to my child?" Chaplain students should also allow families to express their anger at God. Many chaplains are very good as long as the patient displaces his anger onto the hospital administration, nurses, or other members of the helping profession. But as soon as the patient expresses anger at God, they have the need to put the brakes on. I think it is very important that patients are allowed to express their anger at God, and my answer to the chaplain students is always, "Do you really think you have to come to God's defense? I think God can take it. He is bigger than that!"

You have read so far about the "no, not me" stage, the stage of denial, and the "why me?" stage, the stage of anger. The "why me?" stage can also be the "why now?" When you sometimes see old men who have worked all their lives, who have never taken a vacation, who have saved all their money to get the children through school, who finally start to concern themselves with their retirement, and two months before retirement, find that their wives are full of cancer—those people also say, Why me? Why now? Don't I deserve at least a year with my wife in retirement? Wasn't I a good Christian? Wasn't I a good father, a good provider? People need somebody on whose shoulder they can cry and to whom they can say, Why now? Why me? If we can help them to ventilate their feelings of grief, anguish, rage, and anger without judging them, then they will proceed very quickly to a peculiar stage of bargaining. During this time, they have stopped saying, No, not me. They have stopped questioning, Why me? They are now saying, Yes, it's me but. . . . The "but" usually includes a prayer to God—If you give me one more year to live, I'll be a good Christian, or I'll go to the synagogue very day, or I'll donate my eyes or my kidneys. Patients usually promise something, usually in exchange for prolongation of life. It looks like peace, but it is not peace yet; it is a truce, during which time the patient looks rather comfortable, usually requires relatively little pain medication, doesn't call the nursing station all the time—and we often have the delusions that we have done our job. This is only a temporary truce, during which the patient is at relative peace; he feels that he is ready now to face it but asks and hopes for a little extension, usually to finish unfinished business. It is during this time that the patients put their house in order, that they take care of the last will, that they begin to concern themselves with who is taking care of the business or their children. It is usually a bargain with God. The clergy hears most of the bargains. If you do not pay attention to the bargain, you will not hear it.

I will give you a brief example of bargaining, not with God but with a physician. We had a woman who was rather difficult as a patient, avoided by almost everybody. One day she became friendly and asked if I could give her one single day without dependency on injections for pain around the clock—she would be a good patient. This is a very unusual request, because patients usually ask for much more than one day. I asked her why she asked for only one day. She said that she would very much like to spend one day out of the hospital. Her big dream was that she could get dressed up once more, look and feel like a "million dollars." She would like to attend her favorite son's wedding. If she could do that, she would then return to the hospital the same evening and accept whatever would come. We used very extraordinary means to achieve this goal, and this woman was actually able to leave the hospital looking and feeling like a million dollars. She left the hospital for one day. In the evening I waited for her because I wondered what it must be like to ask for only one single day. She saw me in the hallway and greeted me with the words, "Don't forget, Dr. Ross, I have another son."

This is the most typical bargaining. The promises these patients make, they hardly ever keep. Mothers are the most difficult when it comes to bargaining; they very rarely keep their promises. They ask God to allow them to live until the children are out of school. The moment the children are out of school, they add the prayer to stay alive until the children get married and the day of the wedding. Then until they have grandchildren.

Almost everyone bargains with God, even if they have not acknowledged Him before. I'll quote you a few lines from a letter of a young woman who faced her death. She said about her own bargaining with God, "My thoughts were scary, too, not all of love, as loneliness and being alone with death cultivated great bitterness and resentment. So after I argued with the Lord, I called a truce with Him. If He would allow me to accept the present probability with death, I would stop being resentful, stop fighting with Him about His 'making me go.'" I'll give you another example of bargaining, as another illustration of symbolic language.

A twenty-five-year-old man in our hospital was faced with acute leukemia and died two weeks after his hospitalization. He had three little children, all below the age of three, a wife who had no profession and no financial resources, and he appeared to have a terribly difficult time facing his imminent death. I went to see him on several occasions and asked if he felt like talking about it. Each time he gave me the same answer: "Not now, not today, maybe tomorrow." His reason for not being able to talk about it was that his lips were sore and his tongue was sore. I finally thought that this was my problem, because I myself have small children, and maybe it was my need to talk about it. So I went back to his room and I said to him, "Larry, if you never want to talk about it, that's all right, too." He said, "Oh, no, this is not the problem. You don't understand. In this hospital they wake you up in the very early morning hours to take your blood pressure. Then you doze off again. They wake you up again to bring your food tray, and it goes on like this all day long. It is very difficult to have a private conversation when you are interrupted all the time." I asked him how I could help him, and he asked if I could come the next morning very early, before rounds, before anybody else could come into his room, and then he probably could talk about it.

I went back to the hospital the next morning very early. I have a habit of stopping by at the nursing station, where a nurse told me that there was no sense going back into his room because he was in the process of dying. He apparently had put up a big physical fight during the night. He had to be restrained; the priest was called, the physician was called, the family was with him, and the nurse felt that it was too late for him to talk about anything.

I must have been ambivalent about visiting him, because I listened to the nurse. Looking back at this episode a decade ago, I must admit that I have never had a single patient who had set the time and place and even chosen the person with whom to finish unfinished business and who then died prematurely. I took my good old time and about one half hour later I went to his room, only because I promised that I would come back. I expected him to be in a coma. When I opened the door, he sat in his bed more alive, more alert than I had ever seen him before and he looked at me and said, "What took you so long?" I didn't dare tell him!

I closed the door behind me very fast and he invited me to sit down and hurry up in order for him to share what he needed to share with another human being before the next interruption. I sat down and asked him, "What happened to you last night?" He said, "You would never believe what happened to me last night. I put up a big physical fight. There was this big train going rapidly down the hill and I had a big fight and a big argument with the train master. I demanded that he stop this train one-tenth of an inch short! Do you know what I'm talking about?"

This is a typical example of the symbolic-language bargaining with God. I told him that I presumed that the train going rapidly down the hill toward the end was his life and that he had a big argument with God, asking for a tiny little extension of time. He smiled and was just ready to proceed when his mother entered the room.

This is a problem that many of us have: When we are in the midst of talking with our patient, we are interrupted by members of the family, who naturally have a right to be with their dying relatives. In order to continue the dialogue and to finish the unfinished business with Larry, I used his own language, and in front of his mother I said to him, "Larry, how can I help you with a tenth of an inch?" He smiled and said, "I hope that you can help me to convince my mother to go home once more and to bake a loaf of bread and to make my favorite vegetable soup—I always used to love it so much." The mother's response to it was a typical mother's response. She said, "How can I leave my son after a night like this?" And both the patient and I said, as if out of one mouth, "If he thinks he can wait for it, he'll wait for it." Needless to say, the mother did go home, baked a loaf of bread, brought it back to the hospital with his favorite vegetable soup. He was able to eat a little piece of bread and a little bit of the soup—this was the last food he was able to take by mouth. He then slipped into a coma and died about three days later, very peacefully.

Larry is a good example of a young man, aged twenty-five, who had a very short time to come to grips with his own death. I think he died very much as he had lived. He was a big, strong, manly man who tried to maintain denial as long as he could. And then in one night, in three and one-half hours, he went through the stages of rage, anger, bargaining with God, and final acceptance. I'm using these examples to show you how very little time it takes to help these patients to come to grips with death, if you are available to them when they are ready to talk about it and if you do not expect them to communicate their needs to you when it is convenient for you. When a patient has finished the bargaining, he will no longer say "but"—it is then "yes me." That is the stage of depression. Patients then often become very sad and go through two types of depression.

First, they go through a kind of reactive depression in which they mourn past losses, they talk about the meaning of a loss of a breast or a leg, or about the colostomy. They will share with you how difficult it is not to be home with the children, or for a man to give up his job. During this time of depression, we are doing a good job, because all of us have experienced losses and can empathize with our patients. But then our patients go through a different type of depression, which is very difficult to deal with, not only for the family but also for the staff. That is the silent grief or the preparatory grief. During this time they mourn not past losses but future losses. They are beginning to mourn their own death, beginning to be aware of the fact they are losing not one beloved person but all the people and all the things that have meaning to their life. During the silent preparatory grief, they do not talk much anymore; they cannot verbalize their anguish and their sadness; they usually ask for their relatives and acquaintances to come once more and then no more. Then they want to see the children once more, and at the very end they usually like to be with one beloved person or two who can sit silently; the holding of a hand or the touch is more important than words.

It is during this preparatory grief that men have much more difficulty than women, because in our society it is supposed to be unmanly to cry. When one of our patients lies quietly in his pillows and tears are rolling down his cheeks, we become very uncomfortable. We start changing flower arrangements around. We start checking infusions and transfusions that run perfectly well. And if the patient still doesn't talk or move, we often come into the room and say, "Cheer up, it's not so bad!"

Not so bad for whom? is the question! If I were to become a widow, everybody would allow me to grieve and mourn for a whole year over the loss of one person. A man who has the courage to face his own death has the courage to face the loss of everybody and everything that has had meaning to his life—and that is a thousand times more sad. I think we have to allow these people to grieve and cry and not stop their tears, but rather do the opposite. We go into our patients' rooms and say to them, "It takes a man to cry." We allow and encourage them to cry. Those patients do not have to feel unmanly; they do not have to hide their tears. They are then able to go through the preparatory grief much more quickly and are able to reach the last stage, the stage of acceptance.

It is during the preparatory grief that the patient gives us the least problems, although the families are often beginning to get frantic. They will ask the physician to turn the clock back. They will beg the physician for some additional procedures to prolong life. I will give you an example of what happens when a man is able to reach the stage of acceptance but his wife hangs on and implies, "Don't die on me." This makes the dying patient feel guilty, and it is very difficult then to reach a peaceful stage of acceptance. It is also an example of what unfinished business can be all about.

We had a man in his fifties, a dentist, who was dying. He heard from another dying patient about our work and requested a consultation. I went to see him, and he shared with me that he had some unfinished business that he would like to discuss. He was a short, rather skinny, tiny-looking man, and he told me that he had several extramarital relationships he would like to terminate. (My gut reaction to him was *"You?"* because he didn't look like a Don Juan to me!) He then proceeded doing what I tell my students to do; he tried to explain why he did what he did, and that means he tried to understand why he had

44

to have these extramarital relationships rather than to present things in a judgmental manner. He shared with me how he was always a short little boy, how he was raised by his family never to feel like a man, and how his biggest need in life was to prove that he was man enough. It took very little on the part of a woman to smile at him. He would invite her for a cup of coffee, a cup of coffee led to a whiskey sour, and the whiskey sour to the bedroom.

I listened to his confession and asked him why he shared this with me. He said he would like to terminate those relationships and to explain to these women why he did what he did. I made a big mistake at this moment in offering him my help. I said to him, "If you want me to talk to these women, I will be glad to do that." He looked at me with tremendous disappointment and said, "Dr. Ross, I thought you implied that I am man enough."

This is why I say that dying patients are marvelous teachers. When you make a mistake, and you will make many mistakes in this kind of counseling, the patient will most often correct you immediately. If you can take these corrections as lessons and learn from your mistakes, you will learn something about yourself and others with each patient that you counsel.

I told him that this was one of my problems, that sometimes we overdo things, that he was man enough to finish his own unfinished business, and wished him good luck. He was able to terminate these relationships, and he called me again to tell me that he had the toughest job ahead of him now; it was to explain to his wife why he did what he did. Before I could say anything, he put his finger on his lips and said, "Shhh, don't say it." What he tried to imply is, "Don't say now, 'If you want me to talk to your wife, I'll be glad to talk to her.' " I told him that I try not to make the same mistake twice with the same patient, and we were able to have a good laugh together. I told him that I would be available to him if he wanted to see me again. He explained to his wife why he did what he did, and his wife's reaction was, "If you are asking for a divorce, you can have it." I asked Mr. P. how he took that, and I think his appraisal was a very correct one. He said, "I think we are just expecting too much of her. This is beyond her comprehension." He finished his relationships, he explained to his wife why he had done what he did in his life, and he was a proud man. I think for the first time in his life he truly felt like a man.

He was lying in his bed with his eyes closed, very close to death in a stage of peace and acceptance—he was a proud man—when his wife dashed into my office, not even knocking on the door, and yelled at me, "He doesn't talk anymore." I tried to explain to her that her husband had said everything that needed to be said. She became very angry and said," I know all that, but you don't understand. I brought all those relatives from far away, and he could at least say hello to them." This woman obviously could not hear. I thought, maybe she can see; if she sees her husband's peaceful face very close to dying, maybe she'll understand it is too late to be sociable. I walked with her to her husband's room. My initial reaction was to get them all out of the room. But before I could say or do anything, she walked straight over to her husband, pinched him on the cheeks, and said, "Be sociable!" This is both a symbolic, non-verbal gesture of pinching the cheeks and the desperate state-ment, Be sociable. Your gut reaction is probably a very negative one toward the wife, but when you are aware of your negative gut reaction, you always have to ask yourself, What does this woman teach me? This woman in her desperate gesture to her husband, desperately asks, Don't die on me. You have always been the host. You have always taken care of the guests. I haven't even started to conceive that I soon have to take over.

In this case, we did a good job with the patient; we had not done a good job with Mrs. P. If you truly want to help dying patients, you cannot exclude the family. We always try to follow the golden rule to help the ones who limp behind in the stages. If the family can finish their unfinished business before a patient dies, then there is no grief work to do whatsoever after death, although there will always be the natural grief.

The last stage, the stage of acceptance, is perhaps the most difficult to describe. It is a patient who does not want visitors anymore, who does not want to talk anymore, who has usually finished his unfinished business, whose hope is no longer associated with cure, treatment, and prolongation of life. It is a feeling of inner and outer peace. The best description, perhaps, of a patient in the stage of acceptance is conveyed by a patient who wrote:

I have a wonderful husband who I can talk freely with and a couple of sisters, but other than that, the subject of my illness is always a taboo conversation. People shy away from any mention of it. We had a wonderful Christmas, and I am very thankful that after almost two years since the diagnosis, I feel as good as I do. I've been on Prednisone off and on since August and it seems to help temporarily. The overwhelming weakness is the worst, and trying to keep up with five active boys, two and a half years old to eight years old, wears me down very fast . . . but you get a little bit less particular about dust in the corners and you enjoy the boys as they are right now, and not wonder about their future—the Lord will take care of that. There are so many things that I would like to say to them, so I am writing a lot of thoughts down on paper, and someday their dad can read it to them when they are old enough to comprehend the thoughts that I would like to leave with them. We live in such a fast-paced world, very few people really, truly enjoy their everyday living; they are always planning for tomorrow and next year. My husband and I have gone through so much, but we have lived life fully and enjoyed it more than some people in a whole lifetime. A neighbor lady came up to me at the Christmas party, looked me straight in my eyes and said, "How can you be so happy?" I told her that I was happy, and there was no sense in being sad and making everyone around me sad. Depressed feelings still come often—often when we talk about our future years, but I just start thinking about something else or do some sewing for the children. Nobody but the Lord knows for sure . . . so I'm going to enjoy right now!

When a patient has reached the stage of acceptance, that necessarily does not mean that he is close to death. This is something that we could teach our children even before they go to school. The stage of acceptance simply means that people have faced that they are finite, that they live a different quality of life with different values, that they learn to enjoy today and not worry too much about tomorrow, and that they hope that they still have a long, long time to enjoy this kind of life.

I have to say one more word about the differential diagnosis between acceptance and resignation. Acceptance is a feeling of victory, a feeling of peace, of serenity, of positive submission to things we cannot change.

Resignation is more a feeling of defeat, of bitterness, of what's the use, I'm tired of fighting. I would estimate that about 80 percent of our nursing-home patients are in a stage of resignation.

I'll give you a brief clinical example of the differential diagnosis. A few years ago I went to visit an eighty-three-year-old man, a wise old man whom I visited more socially than anything else. When I visited him, he said, "Dr. Ross, there isn't anything you can do for me except pray to the Lord that he takes me soon." I did not really listen to him. I presumed that since he was eighty-three years old, he was in a stage of acceptance and he meant what he said. I visited him for a few minutes and then went home. About a month later, I was called back to Switzerland, where my own mother was close to dying. The only patient I needed to see was this wise old man, obviously to recharge my own battery in the hope that my mother would be in the same stage of acceptance as my old friend. But much to my dismay, he was no longer this calm man, in the peaceful stage of acceptance I needed to see. He greeted me in the hallway with a sense of great urgency and said, "Dr. Ross, did you pray?" I said no and didn't finish the sentence when he interrupted me with, "Thank God! Do you remember the seventy-three-year-old lady across the hall?" He had fallen in love and wanted to live again! He was afraid that I prayed too soon and the Lord took my request seriously! This is a good example of my not listening. If I had listened to him, and when he had said, "Pray to the Lord that he takes me soon," I should have sat down and asked him, "What's your hurry?" and he most likely would have said to me, "What do you mean, what's my hurry? I'm eighty-three years old, I sit here and watch television, maybe I do some occupational therapy projects, but nobody really cares whether I live or die. I might as well die." This is resignation, not acceptance, and it means that we have to help such people find some meaning and purpose in their lives, no matter how limited or restricted they are. Television sets and fancy occupational therapy projects will not replace human needs and human care. A seventy-three-year-old lady gave him the feeling of being needed and wanted and loved again, and he wanted to live again—very much so.

There are many children in our society who have the same needs, and I'm speaking not only of retarded children, of chronically ill or dying children, but also of many children who are in day-care centers and orphanages. My big hope is that nursing-home administrators would consider these needs and build nursing homes with day-care centers on their premises. Those children would then be loved and cared for by the old, lonely people, and this care would give the old people a new purpose and a new meaning in their old age. Instead of watching television, they would be loved by and be busy with the small children. I think many of these old people would then die in a stage of acceptance rather than one of resignation.

Dying Children

For the last few years I have worked almost exclusively with dying children. I think, in general, children would die much more easily than do grown-ups, if we the grown-ups would not make such a mystery of dying. Small children, even three- and four-year-olds, can talk about their dying and are aware of their impending death. It is important that we keep in mind that at such times they most frequently use symbolic verbal and non-verbal language. We are born with only two natural fears, one of falling and one of loud noises. All other fears are unnatural and passed on from fearful adults to children.

When small children are sick or have to be hospitalized, they are most concerned about being separated from their parents. It is our belief that sick children should be allowed to be visited by their parents without any limitations.

When children reach age three or four, in addition to the fear of separation comes a fear of mutilation. This is when they begin to see death in their environment. They may see a car run over a cat or a dog and associate death with a mutilated, horrible body. Or they may see a cat tear up a bird. This also is the time when children become very aware of their bodies and are very proud of them. Little boys discover that they have something that little girls don't have; they want to be big and strong like Superman or like their own daddy. They scream when you have to take blood from them as if you are chopping off their head or their arm. Very often parents bribe their children, promise them all sorts of toys if they don't cry. They thus set a very bad tone especially detrimental to children who have leukemia and similar disorders with remissions and relapses. Children sense very quickly that the louder they cry, the bigger the toy.

We are of the belief that children should be dealt with honestly and openly, that you should not promise them toys for good behavior, that you should tell them it hurts if a procedure is going to hurt. Not only should you tell them what you are going to do with them, but you should also show them. We very often use a doll or teddy bear and allow the children to do the procedure on the teddy bear or the doll, so they know exactly what they have to face. This does not mean that they don't cry when you stick them, or when you have to do bone marrow tests on them, but they know that you have been honest with them and will take the procedure much more easily than if you had lied to them at the beginning of a serious illness.

It is after this fear of separation and mutilation that children begin to talk about death as if death were a temporary happening. This is a very important concept and one that grown-ups should understand better. I think this fear of death as a temporary happening occurs at the same age when children feel very often impotent in the face of a mommy who always says no. They feel angry, enraged, and impotent, and the only weapon that a four- or five-year-old has is to wish mommy to drop dead. This basically means, for a four- or five-year-old, "I'm making you dead now because you are a bad mommy, but two or three hours later when I want a peanut butter and jelly sandwich I will make you get up again and fix it for me." This is what it means to believe in death as a temporary happening. My own child at four years old responded in a similar fashion when we buried a dog in the fall. She suddenly looked at me and said, "This is really not so sad. Next spring when your tulips come up, he'll come up again and play with me." I believe that it is important that we allow children to have this belief although from a scientific point of view this is not correct. It is like telling a child that there is no Santa Claus when he still needs to believe in Santa Claus. As children begin to get a little bit older, they will begin to see death as a permanent happening. They will very often personalize death—in this country it is the "bo-geyman." In Switzerland it used to be a skeleton with a scythe. This is culturally determined. When a child is a little older still, he will begin to believe that death is a permanent happening. After about age eight or nine children see death very much as a permanent happening, just as grown-ups do.

The only exception to this general outline is hospitalized children. Children who are in hospitals for months usually grow up and mature more quickly than do children who live in a protected environment. They often look very young and small physically, but in terms of their concept of their own death they are much more mature than other children. I will give you a brief example of how children mature and grow up quickly when they are in a hospital for several months. It is also an example of how children can talk openly and simply about their own im-pending death, while grown-ups still struggle with how to talk to children about dying.

We had a seven-year-old girl in our hospital who was close to dying of leukemia. As far as the staff was concerned, she asked too many questions, and she often inquired about other children who had died on the floor. The more grown-ups she asked, the more answers she received, and she very quickly picked up that grown-ups have a problem. One day she changed her tactic and made rounds asking the staff what it was going to be like "when I die." Everybody was taken by surprise, and I think each person responded in his own typical fashion. The physician's response was, "I hear my page." We call this avoidance. Avoidance is not helpful, but it is also not destructive. It simply implies, "I'm a busy man, I don't have time to talk about things like this." The little girl did not give up. She cornered the nurse and asked the nurse, "What is it going to be like when I die?" She said, "You are a bad girl. Don't talk like this. Take your medicine and you'll get well." This is a much more detrimental response than the physician's avoidance, because it projects the nurse's own concept of death as a punishment. What it implies basically is that if you are a good girl and do as I tell you, you are going to get well, and if you are a bad girl, you are going to die—which is a lie in the first place. This little girl then asked the chaplain. The chaplain, too, wanted to take off, but he turned around and asked her, "What do you think it is going to be like?" The little girl, relieved that somebody wasn't avoiding her question, said to him, "I think what's going to happen is that I'm going to fall asleep one of these days and when I wake up, I'm with Jesus and my little sister." The chaplain responded, "This must be very beautiful," which she acknowledged and hopped off and went back to play.

I'm not saying that all children respond that maturely and without fear to their own death, but I think we can presume that this little girl was raised in a family of love and faith and in an environment that accepted death as part of life. It is important that we raise our children teaching them that death is part of life. If we do this before they go to school, these children will never have to go through the stages we have outlined before.

Parents often go through all the stages when they are faced with the impending death of a child, and I think grown-ups have a much more difficult time accepting the death of a beloved child. It is important that we spend all our effort in helping these parents, preferably before a child dies, so they may at least reach some degree of acceptance. I will share with you one of my most precious possessions, which perhaps best describes what parents go through when they are faced with the probability of the death of one of their children. This was a birthday present given to me by a mother of a child with leukemia.

I had counseled both parents for about a year. Each time the mother felt she had made some progress, she was able to write down in the form of a poem what she went through. I will simply reproduce these poems for you and make some commentary at the end of each one. Her first poem is dedicated to her son's roommate, who was also dying of leukemia. It is called "A Fun Day at the Leukemia Clinic":

A child near death I saw today
His smile too slow, his face too gray.
His gaze not here but far away
And I wondered, tomorrow mine this way?

I hold my own and give him a kiss
His grinning return leaves a feeling of bliss
So I almost believe there is nothing amiss,
Please let him always stay just like this.

He's warm and alive and eager to smile
Jumping and hopping and running a mile.
An innocent babe without cunning or guile.
All I ask is to keep him just for a while.

Who is to stay and who is to go?
Until the last moment, who is to know?
There is no rhyme or reason, what is must be so,
But I'm screaming inside—never mine—never no!!

This is a poem describing a partial denial. She knows intellectually that it is going to happen to her child, but deep down inside she cannot believe, and she says "never mine—never no!" Her next poem is again to her boy's roommmate, entitled "Please Die Soon":

He is eight years old though he looks much more,
He has been kept too long in front of death's door.
I wonder how long before he dies,
He's a ghastly preview before our eyes.

I think of my own and what I will do
And what I can give when this hell he goes through
I'm scared when I cry—I don't want him to go
But damn it if he must—let it not be so slow.

A child should die not so slowly it seems
It shouldn't be pain & suffering & screams.
Let him die as he has lived, laughing his life along
When mine goes—if he goes—let him leave with a song.

And the next poem, entitled "To Kenny—Goodbye with Love":

You left us last night and quickly so
I guess you knew it was time to go.
Better than those who would have to stay
For one more hour or another day.

It was time to leave, while you still could be
Though physically bound, in spirit free.
You still could smile and still could sing,
Still could do so many things.

There are some battles that can't be won
The fight was hard but now it's done.
You fought so well and gave your best
And now, dear Kenny, it's time to rest.

Do you feel a degree of acceptance in the face of Kenny's death? This mother does with Kenny what we are doing with our own patients. If you cannot face your own death, it is conceivable that you can't accept your patients' deaths. Each time you dare to get truly involved with your patients and reach a stage of acceptance, it will help you to come a step closer toward acceptance of your own finiteness. This mother did the same thing with Kenny. She could not accept her own child's death yet, but she was able to accept Kenny's death. This will help her to face her own little boy's death. She tries it with other children. She writes a poem to Beth, called "Happy Birthday Nine Year Old":

Nine should be happy and ready to run
Playing with dolls, having all sorts of fun
Or setting your hair in a fancy new way
Giggling with friends and talking all day.

But not lying here in a hospital bed
With needles in arm and no hair on your head.
It seems somehow fitting and I think I know why
In a hospital born—now come back to die.

In this poem she apparently tries to make sense out of all this nonsense. She then moves from the denial to the stage of rage and anger. She displaces this anger onto many people, onto the hospital staff. I'll quote just a few lines of one of the poems, called "Song of the Intern": "I'm the intern big and strong/ Believe me I can do no wrong./ I do things quick—I do things fast/ Who care if things are done half *$¢%!/ Tomorrow maybe I'll practice on you,/ Bone marrows, shots, an I.V. or two./ In a couple of years I'll really know how,/ You'll just have to bear with my clumsiness now."

She is now angry at anybody who touches her little boy, and only after she has gone through weeks of anger displaced onto many people. She is now going to the grief period, and she tries to begin to conceive of what it is like when her little boy is actually dead. Her little boy's name is Jeff, and you have to know his name in order to hear how she tries to conceive of it prior to his death. The poem is called "Hospital Playroom":

Come to the playroom and look inside
See all the toys of the children who have died.
There is Beth Ann's doll and a book from Mary
A bat and a ball and a mitt from Larry.

Kenny's crayons are used each day,
And the coloring book belonged to Kay.
Boxes of toys and boxes of joys
That's all that's left of the dead girls and boys.

I wonder what of Jeffy's we'll give
To this graveyard that said these children lived.
A puzzle, a book or his shiny new bike.
His fire engine or the red old trike.

It's supposed to be fun to come here and play
With a sick little child made happy today.
But my eyes and my heart from this place want to go
It's filled with the ghosts of the children we know.

When she has gone through this preparatory grief, she is now very close to the stage of acceptance, which is very hard for her to find because she has no concept of any form of life after death. She is a woman without any formal religious beliefs and she believes that when you are dead you are dead—there is no heaven, no form of immortality. Therefore, it is very difficult for her to understand what is going to happen to her little Jeff. She writes a poem to him entitled "Where Are You Going, My Little One?":

I saw a boy on a bike go by
He was ten years old and blue of eye.
Slender like you with straight blond hair
But hard as I looked, you were not there.

A group of children playing ball
Boys and girls both big and small.
I was restless inside and the panic grew,
Because try as I might, I could not see you.

You are not really one of them, my little son
You'll always be a special one.
Here a short while, then gone somewhere
I could rest inside if I just knew where.

I glanced up at the clouds as they billowed by
Floating free in a peaceful sky
Lovely and light—they have not a care
And finally my son, I found you there.

I hope that you can see the picture of the eight-year-old who, reaching the stage of acceptance, drew a peace bird flying up into the sky. This is a similar symbol of peaceful acceptance to that used by this mother when she says, "I glanced up at the clouds as they billowed by/ Floating free in a peaceful sky/ Lovely and light—they had not a care/ And finally my son, I found you there." She then writes a poem about the future:

> I cram it all in now as much as I can
> For today is tomorrow for our little man.
> Make memories now and hold them fast
> For the future is but a thing of the past.
>
> The feeling of panic is slow to leave
> I spent so much time getting ready to grieve.
> Why is he going . . . does nothing last?
> The future should not be a thing of the past.
>
> But some songs are short and some are long
> Four years of perfection but still a short song.
> But today he does sing and he's lively and loud
> And the future has become the present—the now.

After the mother reached the stage of acceptance and learned to enjoy today and not think too much about tomorrow, little Jeff picked up very quickly that his mother was able to talk about it. He started to talk about his own death, as expressed in a poem entitled "Where Did Kenny Go?":

> Mommy, where did Kenny go
> He was my friend and I liked him so.
> It has been a long time since I've seen him
> And I can't figure out where he's been.
>
> Kenny died?
> Who killed him, Mom?
> I wonder—was it a gun or a bomb?
>
> Oh, nobody killed him
> He had been so sick
> That his body wouldn't work
> And he died very quick.
>
> Just like Ma and Daddy and you
> And Grandpa and Shadows too.

Where was he, Mommy, when he got dead?
Was he playing at home or somewhere in bed?

I really liked Kenny and I'll miss him a lot
But nothing bad happened, he didn't get shot.
He only did die like we all do someday.
So long, Mommy, I'm going out to play.

I hope that you noted his concept of death as a catastrophic, destructive happening when he said, "Kenny died?/ Who killed him, Mom?/ I wonder—was it a gun or a bomb?" And when his mother saw it as a noncatastrophic happening, he said very quickly, "But nothing bad happened, he didn't get shot./ He only did die like we all do someday./ So long, Mommy, I'm going out to play." Did any of you listen to his last unfinished business and his last concern? He asked, "Where was he mommy when he got dead?/ Was he playing at home or somewhere in bed?" This is a question: Are you going to ship me off to the hospital again or am I going to be allowed to die at home? Little Jeff knew very well that when he was going to be close to death he would be sent to the hospital as most of our patients are.

It was only a few weeks later that Jeff developed pneumonia and started to talk about his impending death again. He suddenly said to his mother, "You know, Mommy, I feel so sick now that I think this time I'm going to die." A year ago his mother would most likely have said to him, "Shut up, don't talk like this, you are going to get well." This time she was able to hear him. She was able to sit down and say to him, "What do you think this is going to be like?" The little four-year-old responded, "I think what's going to happen to me is that you are going to take me in an ambulance from the hospital to the place where Beth Ann is." Beth Ann was the girl who had died a few months earlier and who was at the cemetery, a word little Jeff probably did not know. Then Jeff added: "Yes, I think you'd better make sure and tell someone to put on the light in the ambulance and make the siren go very loud so that Beth Ann knows I'm coming." This to me is one of the most beautiful examples of how small children between the ages of three and five are able to talk about their own death—if we can face it and if we do not avoid the issue.

Jeffy lived until after his ninth birthday, just as unconsciously predicted in the mother's poem, "I saw a boy on a bike go by. . . ." Jeff's one big wish, to be able to go around the block on his shiny new, yet old bike, was fulfilled briefly before his death. He asked his parents to put training wheels on it, and, almost like a drunken man, because of his brain involvement, he was able to ride around the block.

When exhausted, he returned to his bedroom. His parents removed the training wheels, brought the beloved bicycle upstairs to his bedroom—on his request—and left him alone. It was only after his precious possession received a beautiful new shine and wax that he asked his younger brother to visit him in his room and presented the bicycle to him as an early birthday gift. Jeffy died a couple of weeks later, proud that he had achieved what he always wanted and even happier that he was able to pass his beloved bicycle on to his brother, who was healthy enough, and by now seven years old, so he could master it without training wheels.

These apparently insignificant things are most important and belong to the unfinished business that young children have to complete before they are able to let go.

I had another mother, whose boy died at age twelve, who was convinced that he did not talk about dying. It was only after his death, with our help, that she was able to find a poem that the twelve-year-old wrote one year prior to his death. I print this poem to show you how very mature and grown-up some of these children are when they talk in their own language about their impending death, which grown-ups do not want to hear about. He wrote a poem entitled "The Flame":

> The flame is like a human,
> It lives and dies.
> Its life is a wild impetuous one
> During its span—it frolics dances and
> Appears to have a carefree existence.
> Although it might be joyous in a short period
> It has a tragic death
> The tragedy is in its struggle not to die.
> But first the flame casts an eery bluish magnetism
> Just as it's about to let go, it flickers and springs
> Back to life again.
> At that moment it appears that the vital desire
> For survival will be the victor.
> But neither flame nor human is destined for eternal life
> Death is near—the flame sputters as it reaches out to
> grasp on to a dangling string, trying to resist its
> overshadowing fate—but to no avail . . .
> Death has exhausted its opposition
> And conquered!

This is the language of a twelve-year-old a year before his death. My hope is that more parents are aware that children can and will talk about their impending death, that they will help parents to face their death, and that we do not avoid the issue but rather teach it to young children years before they have to face their own death. If we could do that, we would not need specialists on death and dying, patients would not have to be so terribly isolated in our hospital wards, and we could finally face up to the fact that we all have to die sooner or later.

We have worked with dying patients over the past decade and have spent much time with parents and siblings of dying children. With the brief moments that each one of us has between the diagnosis of a terminal illness or an accident and the actual death of a patient, time has often been a problem. Many therapists and physicians simply stay away from such "clients" because they are concerned that counseling such a family would require too much time. This is really not correct. We have referred earlier to the use of symbolic language and the need to teach and learn this art of communication and interpretation whenever possible.

It is with the help of a technique developed at the Kantonsspital in Zurich, where I studied medicine, that we have been able to understand the comprehension of illness, trauma, and impending death in young children. We have used this simple and non-time-consuming method in helping siblings (case of L.) and children of dying parents (cases of D. and B.) to express their concerns and their concepts, in order to better assist them in a crisis situation in which there is not much time for longer counseling.

Since practically no literature is available about this approach, I would like to present a brief outline of the method of collecting and analyzing such data. I have asked Dr. Gregg Furth, a student of mine, to summarize his experiences, as his time spent with Susan Bach in England has given him more expertise in this field than anyone else working currently in the United States.

II

THE USE OF DRAWINGS MADE AT SIGNIFICANT TIMES IN ONE'S LIFE

BY GREGG M. FURTH, PH. D.

EVERY ARTIST uses his medium to reflect and comment upon the world in which he lives. The world is seen and experienced differently by everyone, and each artist, as we might expect, reflects and comments upon a different aspect of the world. A soup can painted by Andy Warhol reflects values and attitudes about art and society that are quite different from the ones expressed by Michelangelo's *The Last Judgment*. These nonverbal "commentaries" record both conscious and unconscious impressions that come from the artist.

We receive from the child a picture of his world that is often clearer and more direct than what the artist portrays, because the child has little formal knowledge of art. When a child is investing his feelings and ideas in his drawing, the process unfolds without any critical forces to accuse him, e.g., that his tree is not drawn well or that a tree has been drawn this way before. When a child draws a tree, for him it is a tree; if we do not recognize it as such, the child will happily tell us what it is. It appears that the child's feelings and thoughts (conscious and unconscious) flow freely and directly onto the drawing paper.

In essence, we are dealing with the child's drawing without considering aesthetics, and we find his picture of the world to be less veiled in the formal elements of technique. The child's decision about what to draw and how to draw it frequently provides a clear representation of his impressions that go unexpressed on the conscious level.

One thing we can conclude relative either to analyzing scribbled doodles for meaning or to criticizing "serious" art is that nonverbal acts communicate feelings and thought, coming from both one's conscious and unconscious functioning. Let us consider how this functioning serves a seriously ill child who chooses to draw a picture. A large part of the child's world now circles around his diseased body, so we might expect to find in his drawing many references to his illness. If a dying child draws a picture, we may find that his drawing expresses remarkable acknowledgments and emotions that can alert us to unmet needs or assure us of the child's inner peace. The discoveries of his anxieties, desires, or realizations can help those in contact with him to respond appropriately and minister to his profound needs as a dying child. In a sense, the drawing allows the child the freedom to diagnose himself, and it is left to others to provide the psychological support to lessen any fear or confusion that he feels. But does this diagnosis relate to the child's physical condition as well as to the psychological one?

Until this point I have suggested that a child records in his extemporaneous drawings his unverbalized feelings and thoughts. Such information is useful to all people in contact with the dying child. However, let me also suggest that in another sense the child draws a medical record of himself that might be useful to the caring staff involved in his treatment. In other words, the child's drawing can be a picture of his physical as well as his psychological condition.

Susan Bach, a London psychoanalyst, has studied the spontaneous drawings of terminally ill children. Dr. Bach has focused upon the relationship between the body (soma) and soul (psyche). She contends that the psyche and soma act conjointly to serve the life and health of the individual. If she is correct in seeing this link between psyche and soma, then we should find this link expressed in the undirected, impromptu drawings of children. If the drawings record the child's psychological and spiritual condition and there is a link between psyche and soma, then the physical condition must also be evident in these drawings. Why insist upon the importance of this link between psyche and soma? If we can interpret the drawing as showing this link, then we can use the drawing in treating the whole individual body and personality. Such an inclusive approach should help assure the dying individual the completeness in life that he needs and desires at the approach of death.

I have seen children and adults reach the state in which their soma and psyche are in harmony. It is these dying people whose lives end serenely with a sense of fulfillment and meaning. The dying child can have this sense of completeness even if it remains unexpressed in adults' terms. I believe that it is the dying patient's right to expect others to help him reach as complete a life as he possibly can while he enters the terminal stage of living. This means that this expectation is also the dying child's right. Unexpressed needs must be recognized and met. It is my conviction that drawings can communicate these unspoken wants, needs, and anxieties.

Originally my research was with leukemic children who were terminally ill, and one hypothesis was that the drawings of dying children would be measurably different from those of healthy individuals. While I found this hypothesis supported, I additionally observed evidence of the psyche reflected in the drawings of well children. My research suggested that physically healthy individuals who are expressing some emotional stress do also reveal significant information in extemporaneous drawings. (This is not too surprising, considering that Dr. Bach's research in drawing analysis initially concentrated upon psychiatric patients who were without organic illness.)

I will show in the following case histories how I have used information gained from drawings by physically healthy individuals as well as from drawings by patients with critical, organic diseases. These examples demonstrate the value of drawings for communicating conscious and unconscious information (whether coming from healthy or seriously ill persons). We will see evidence that such drawings have the potential to promote constructive coping. Understanding how to "read" and use these diagnostic drawings is necessary in order for their useful potential to be realized. Such understanding naturally requires much dedicated study and experience.

People often ask me whether this kind of analysis of drawings applies only to children. Adults can be encouraged to draw extemporaneously too, even though they may at first feel more inhibited than a child in complying with this request. Adults' pictures reflect the psyche/soma condition no less than children's pictures do. But in a sense, there is a child in every adult who enters into the adult's drawing. This may be the "wounded child" from years ago who has never received the love and forgiveness needed to enable the individual to recover sufficiently to live the life he is meant to live. Or this "child" may represent an undeveloped potential, whether it be negative or positive, psychological or somatic, that is preparing the individual for its eventual emergence.

All of us in the field of thanatology are working to help those who are dying to enjoy the best quality of life possible in the amount of time they have left. What do we do to help those whose life goes on, to live it more completely? The thanatologist cannot serve exclusively the God of Death; the thanatologist is called upon to serve both the God of Life and the God of Death. The living ones need help to celebrate the life that is here and now.

My task, and that of my colleagues, is to use the pictures

drawn at crucial times in the lives of either children or adults in order to identify and help provide the assistance these individuals need to restore harmony between the body and soul. In addition to the therapeutic gain that individuals may receive from their drawings, these drawings sometimes provide tremendous help for parents or other loved ones, as we will see in some of the following examples.

Laura

The first drawing we will examine comes from Laura, a 30-year-old woman from New York City who was studying at a large university in the East. She was in the process of designing a research project for her doctoral dissertation in psychology when she attended a workshop I taught that concentrated upon interpretation of extemporaneous drawings. Laura's purpose for being at the workshop was "academic." She was going to ask children and adults to draw, as part of her research design, and hoped to gain some insight on how to interpret their drawings. She told me later that upon being asked at my workshop to draw a picture, she resented the request. She explained that she felt uncomfortable approaching this assignment; but being honest with herself she realized that very soon she would be asking people to draw as part of her own research. Therefore, trusting the old adage that "what is good for the goose is good for the gander," she made a drawing and presented it to me (see Figure 1). Although a variety of colored pencils was available, Laura used only her black ball-point pen and held herself in reserve, perhaps not willing to reveal the "true colors" of her personality.

I had talked earlier with Laura and learned about the research project she was designing involving drawings. I judged her to be a very intelligent and perceptive young woman, and did not realize that she doubted the valid use of drawings or would feel uncomfortable at the request to draw.

Let us first look at what Laura's picture may represent psychologically; then we will look at its somatic implications. The drawings was intended to portray Laura in the room where she was sitting. However, there were over sixty people in this room that was crowded for its size, and yet her drawing portrays no other human figure. Also, this drawing is a picture of her present situation, the immediate reality that she is experiencing. My workshop participants were allowed to draw anything they chose. Could it be of some significance that Laura chose to picture her immediate present? What could be so important about the present? What had not been happening that Laura wished would happen? The title she gives the picture, *Beginnings of Peace*, gives us some clues that her past was probably not peaceful, but that a more hopeful way has just begun for her. I wonder what recent change may have occurred in Laura's life to bring about the beginnings of peace.

Looking at the couch in the drawing, we see that it is not grounded; furthermore, it has only one armrest, which is at the end where we notice Laura, snuggled into its corner. What happened to the other end of the couch—why is there no armrest for support? Does this defective sofa suggest that some part of Laura lacks support? This nonsupportive end of the sofa is important to consider because it is so central in the positioning of this drawing. Dividing the picture into quadrants (Figure 2) clearly reveals how this section of the couch is what is centered in this picture. This positioning alerts us to what issue may be of central significance in the life of the individual who drew the picture. We may gather further evidence about this central issue by noticing that not only is the couch without any grounding, but no one is seated with Laura. On the one hand it may be fortunate that this side is left empty, because to be seated beside Laura may not be entirely safe or comfortable. On the other hand, the empty side of the sofa indicates Laura's isolation, which might be unfortunate for her. She is very alone in this picture. At first glance I am not sure how to interpret this loneliness, but since Laura selected to draw a couch with seating capacity for more than one, instead of a chair with single seating, I may suspect that Laura is feeling the loneliness of her situation. Laura's clinging to the end of the couch that has a support causes me to wonder what actual support this woman has been depending upon, and whether it has fallen down or for some reason is not altogether accessible to her now.

Considering that the couch is where Laura is located and that it represents Laura's life, so to speak, it appears that there has been a falling apart of her life and the support system within. Psychologically, this could be very positive. We may find this representing a kind of death and rebirth in her life, symbolizing an initiation into a new phase of life. This calls to mind the necessary falling apart or "death" of one's self before integration and rebirth appears. I refer to the two complementary phases of disintegration and reintegration. In this light, Laura's words, "beginnings of peace," seem particularly significant of reintegration that may have already begun.

Looking closely at the human figure, I wonder whether it is male or female. There is no indication of breasts and I do not observe other feminine characteristics. I question whether Laura is fully conscious of the feminine side of her personality. Contrary to feminine characteristics, I see very solid shoulders and wonder why there is a need for such strong shoulders. Does this person carry a demanding responsibility or heavy burden that would require such strength? Could it be that Laura may realize the responsibility involved in filling the traditional roles of womanhood—e.g., being a wife, mother, and herself—and has yet no way of dealing with what all this may mean to her?

The smile on her face looks forced to me. If one needs to force such a smile, it suggests that she really isn't happy; and this burden she carries may need to be held inside (alone). Consequently, a phony front is put forward for others to see, and Laura's need for broad shoulders to carry the weight of her burden increases.

We observe that the figure's right hand is positioned on the couch's armrest while her left hand covers her genital area. Aristotle once said that the hand is "the tool of tools." So what may these tools do for Laura? One tool helps to steady herself and I wonder if the other one protects her.

This figure with no sexual definition makes me question Laura's attitudes toward sexual intercourse. Is she afraid of her instinctual, female side? Does she fear being loved by a man and giving of herself in order to find herself?

As we look further, we see there is no grounding under her feet or under the couch; she appears to be suspended or floating. What has happened to her base of support and her grounding with reality? Regardless, "beginnings of peace" are there, so I believe something must be developing to give Laura this optimistic attitude. And whatever positive thing is emerging may provide her with a strong foundation to stand upon.

Lastly, I want to look toward the upper half of this picture. Laura informed me that four windows are what we see extending from one side of the paper to the other. I am told that outside the windows there are indications of a rising sun, trees and shrubbery. These objects are not drawn distinctly and look chaotic. Again, looking for the possible meaning of Laura's pictorial language, we surmise that her outer life could be following a pattern of chaos, with loneliness occupying her inner life. However, plants and sun are very positive life signs, indicative of potential growth. Therefore, I conclude that Laura's outer growth—her responses to the world and those about her—will blossom and become fruitful.

On the other hand, if this picture represents a totality of

Laura, then the outdoor scenes of plant life with a rising sun, placed into four sections, call to mind nature's four seasons. Could it be that Laura's four seasons—infancy, childhood, young adulthood, mature adulthood—are in need of growth? Perhaps Laura's discovery of her feminine stance and great potential of her womanhood will provide her needed grounding and support. I have been told that these four sections are windows and I think about the glass in these windows. Glass can symbolize purity, spiritual perfection, or the Great Spirit. So now I am eager to discover what might have happened to Laura in the spiritual realm to cause chaos in her "four seasons."

I learned about Laura's interesting background. She was the second oldest child in a family of eight children. She had been a Catholic nun for nine years. After a tremendous amount of consideration, she left her order. She writes:

As the person who drew this picture, I am very aware of how accurate a reflection this drawing was of how I was feeling at that time. Just about one year into an extensive psychoanalytic psychotherapy, I was becoming aware of the extent of the despair, pessimism, alienation, and sexual inhibition that had characterized my life up to that time. Busily occupied with a full-time psychotherapy internship, a part-time psychology assistantship, doctoral classes in psychology, and work on my thesis, I presented a competent smiling picture of myself to those around me, but was acutely aware of feeling that I had no time for myself. As I struggled with my feelings of being unlovable, I did at least have the support of feeling that I was beginning to find myself professionally.

We have considered many possible psychological dimensions of Laura's drawing and now we will look for possible somatic implications. Looking at this picture again, I now ask, Why does Laura need to protect her genital area? Will Laura experience a somatic process that will require strong shoulders to hold up under the stress? Laura explained to me later that she intended to portray the figure's left hand resting on the thigh, but said, "As I made the drawing it was as if 'involuntarily' my hand ended up protecting my genital area. I distinctly remember being surprised that I could so 'misjudge' the distance I'd intended to move the pen."

One year later, Laura went to her gynecologist for a routine examination and was informed that the Pap smear indicated dysplasia and carcinoma in situ. It was classified as a Type IV smear. Culposcopy results ruled out the possibility of an out-patient biopsy, and Laura was admitted to the hospital for a cone biopsy along with ureteral dilation and cauterization. The results of the biopsy, carcinoma in situ, established a need for protection. Looking back to the picture sometime later, I realized that Laura was sitting on the steadiest part of the couch, and was so close to the stable end that she even appeared to be part of it. Did something in Laura know not only of the need for protection, but did this "something within" also know that everything would be all right if she could just "hold on"?

Bill

Here we have a picture, reluctantly drawn, which nevertheless provided forecasting signs of the person's psychological and somatic development.

Sometimes it is not at all clear what a drawing represents, and this ambiguity may be further complicated by the fact that the individual does not verbalize much about his drawing, thoughts, or feelings. Bill, a hospitalized eight-year-old, presented drawings to me that were more complex and problematic in terms of interpretation than what we saw with Laura's drawing. I met Bill when I was collecting data for my doctoral dissertation. He drew only three pictures for me, each drawn several weeks apart. Most of his comments were made about the first picture (Figure 3).

This first drawing looked somewhat like a butterfly. He described it as "bubbles." A chain of bubbles runs vertically down the middle, separated in the center by a cross. Two large bubbles fill the center horizontally, also separated by the same central cross. There are four isolated bubbles in each corner. The bubbles in the upper two corners became "bubbles inside of flowers" as the drawing progressed. Bill stated that these four corner bubbles were "separate . . . apart and trying to reach over to one another." Concerning the dark-colored bubbles lined vertically above and below the central cross, he commented while coloring them that it was now "like dirt clogging it up and it can't go to the thing [indicating the central cross] . . . so the bubbles can't reach the other bubbles." The bubbles in the lower corners are "floating in water and trying to get out of it." When asked whether he thought the bubbles would get out, he replied, "They might."

It was a frustration and sadness to me that I was restricted from discussing details of physical illness among those patients with whom I visited, although I was permitted to allow the patients to discuss their pictures. I knew that Bill had leukemia and that his case was incurable. I believe that Bill was symbolically describing his illness to me, using his pictures and comments concerning the bubbles. Could these bubbles he mentioned represent his blood cells? Could the clogging action he referred to suggest the spread of cancer cells?

In my opinion, Bill knew of his illness and wanted very much to discuss it, but unfortunately, as I mentioned earlier, the hospital forbade me in my role as a researcher to engage in such discussion. Nevertheless, we talked continually at this pictorial level, and I discovered that the central cross was the cause for all the blockage in this picture. This cross may represent God, and Bill could be blaming God for what is happening to him.

Bill did not want to offer much information about his next

two drawings. He described the second drawing he did for me as wallpaper for his room at home (see Figure 4).

Notice the similar cross in the center, with a flower on each of the four ends. While I observed him drawing this, I was much impressed by the great force he used in making his lines. He held his pencil as though it were a knife or dagger that he was jabbing into something. This alone confirmed for me that Bill desperately needed someone to talk with concerning his situation. Was he experiencing anger toward God?

I discussed my observations with the social worker, who was a very effective member of the hospital staff. She agreed that Bill needed help, but the physician in charge would not consent to write the necessary referral to the hospital child psychiatrist. Consequently, Bill was left alone, quite possibly feeling as "separate" and "apart" as the bubbles in his first picture.

These two pictures indicate that Bill does not choose representational figures as a means of communication in his drawing. By substituting abstract design for representational art or realism, Bill implies he is avoiding or covering up his problems. In my empirical observations of a person's drawings, I find that abstract drawings frequently parallel a period in the individual's life when he is not wishing to face reality, or else prefers to deny it altogether.

Bill did not really want to speak about his second and third drawings (Figures 4 and 5); and I detected that he learned from his parents that he should not discuss his illness. His parents were in the process of obtaining a divorce, and this poor child was lost in the shuffle of parental trauma with no one to show him it was all right to have the thoughts he had and to speak about them as well. Fortunately, he had the drawings to allow at least some of his feelings to surface; yet I do not feel that this activity alone was adequate. Bill was a bright boy who could have articulated his thoughts and feelings if only given the opportunity, permission, and freedom to express those parts of himself that begged to be made known and dealt with. Bill could see and feel that he was not getting well. He was old enough to be aware of the finality of death. Children his age who face death are usually much more disturbed by thoughts of separation from loved ones that the moment of death will bring than they are about the actual process of dying. This separation anxiety was most probably intensified by the separation and impending divorce of his parents.

Bill's third picture (Figure 5) was very frightening to me. He drew, beginning from the lower left corner, making large, sweeping strokes dividing the paper into triangular shapes, and moved toward the upper right corner. He made sixteen segments but did not quite reach the upper right corner. One edge of the top, sixteenth triangle was not completed. Bill began coloring all the triangular shapes, beginning once again with the lower left corner, moving toward the upper right one. I sat quietly while he filled in his page. As he came closer to the end, I became concerned, wondering whether he was filling in his total life. Was there no room for him to change, to grow, or to live? But as he approached the top right corner he stopped and left the incompleted triangular section colorless. He looked thoughtfully at the drawing, picked up the red pencil, and, skipping an open space, he colored the top right corner, then proudly handed his picture to me.

Months later, I found it very striking and remarkable that Bill died sixteen weeks after making this drawing—a time period coinciding with the exact number of triangular units coming up to the empty space. Could it be that "something" inside of Bill knew when he would meet death?

At the time I collected this drawing I was even more convinced that this child should see a counselor, so again I spoke with the social worker. At last the social worker was successful in obtaining for this boy a referral to be seen by the child psychiatrist. How important it is for physicians themselves to recognize the value of diagnosing and treating the psyche and soma together.

Bill refused to draw any more pictures for me after making this third drawing with the sixteen triangular sections. This last drawing showed that he still could not openly communicate about his situation; the only pictures he could give us of his world were ones submerged in abstract representations. But by delving into his abstract pictures we can uncover clues about his somatic and psychological condition.

In his first drawing, anxiety about his disease and the threat of death seem evident. Similarity between his purple bubbles and diseased bone marrow is striking. The bubbles could also be considered as bubbles of trapped air, representing, among other things, the closing off of the breath of life. The bubbles may also suggest, on the psychological side, Bill's relationship with others. Like the bubbles, Bill was unable to reach others; he could not communicate in a direct and conscious way. In a spiritual sense, the bubbles could refer to one's spirit or soul that feels isolated. It is remarkable to see that a cross occupies the center position in both Figures 3 and 4. A cross and flowers often connote the church, God, a cemetery, and death. It seems that this child carried within himself many unanswered questions. We do not know how much stress was added to his life by his parents' broken marriage. I venture to say, however, that this child bore psychological wounds and pain equal to his physical discomfort. Paraphrasing Bill's own words, it is possible to say that he felt confused and "clogged" emotionally, that he wanted to "reach" out for help and "get out of" his pool of confusion, but that he felt "blocked." Quite possibly he perceived that an all-powerful God was responsible for blocking the way to health and happiness, and the cross may have become Bill's cross—his place of suffering.

I can only hope that the child psychiatrist who was finally called was able to bring some healing to this child's wounded spirit. We recall that when Bill was asked whether he thought the bubbles would get out, he replied, "They might."

Nonphysicians in health-care positions who understand the holistic approach to healing have a tremendous responsibility to assist physicians in acknowledging the psyche side and ministering not only to the physical need but to the whole individual.

Teresa

Now we will focus our attention upon a series of drawings I collected from a little girl who had leukemia. When I first saw six-year-old Teresa, she walked into the hospital with her mother. They had traveled quite far to come here for Teresa's treatment. I remember how impressed I was with the mother's warmth and cheerfulness. I observed that Teresa was shy and small for her age. Her face was puffed beyond its normal size owing to fluid accumulation caused by her chemotherapy. She did not talk much, but her smile amply compensated for her reticence. It was easy to read her feelings just by following her expressions. When Teresa did talk, it was about her two sisters and three brothers and the fun they had together watching their favorite TV programs. Her chief joy was her family and the love they gave to her. Teresa would consider it a great sadness to have no one to play with; but with such a large and loving family this calamity was not likely to occur.

Figure 6 is the first of a series of three drawings by Teresa, which appear to be self-portraits. Almost all the leukemic children in my study drew figures that seemed to relate strongly to themselves.

In Figure 6, we see a smiling girl standing on some kind of a base. I had observed how special Teresa seemed to her entire family, so I knew that in actuality there was firm support for this child. Notice that the legs, arms, body, and head are in fairly normal proportion to one another, and that the face is very round. But what especially absorbs my interest is the way that the tips of her toes and the top of her head form a connecting link between the ground and the sky. How can such a little one be touching both heaven and earth? Could we take this to indicate that her time is near? The next picture may give us more insight.

When Teresa arrived a month later at the clinic, she drew the picture we see in Figure 7. We learned that she was experiencing pain in her legs at this time. She commented that her drawing was her backyard and that the girl had been picking flowers. There were twelve flowers shown. I notice that the picture is symmetrical, with a tree on both sides, five flowers suspended on each side, and each hand holding one flower. Why should there be a total of twelve flowers? Repeated objects often relate to a significant period of time in one's life (see the sixteen triangular sections in Bill's drawing, Figure 5). What I find frightening, however, is the repositioning of the blue sky: In the first drawing it touches Teresa's head, but in Figure 7 it becomes her grounding. To have "heaven above" is grand—all is in its place. But "heaven below" makes me concerned for the future. Is this movement of color just a childish whim? I don't think so.

Notice how the figure's legs are spindlier than in the former drawing, and that the face is out of proportion to the body. However, the smile on the face is still Teresa's smile.

After two months, Teresa returned to the clinic, this time on crutches. Her legs were giving her severe pain and she had difficulty moving them. She drew another picture for me (see Figure 8).

The outdoor scene is gone now, and the figure's moon-shaped face occupies much of the page. Once again we see a reflection of the results of her chemotherapy. Not only had the drugs caused puffy edema to alter her appearance, but they had made her hair fall out as well. The arms and legs are very small extensions on this figure's body. In reality, Teresa's own limbs were small and useless. In fact, one week later, Teresa was carried into the hospital by her mother, and within a few weeks the child died.

It is interesting to note that whether by accident or coincidence—whichever one chooses to call it—twelve weeks after Teresa made her drawing containing the twelve flowers, she died.

Let us look again at Teresa's three extemporaneous drawings and compare them. Teresa's treatment of the figure's arms and legs show her actual prognosis of immobility before she became immobile. Following the series, we see that her body recedes in size, until her face is almost top-heavy, with the body too small to support her head. There is an interesting detail that appears in the last picture. Instead of one dot for a nose, the figure has two, representing nostrils. Teresa seems to be communicating to us her own awareness that her body is less supportive, and that she is focusing more on breath itself to stay alive. The smile remains on the figure. I have no reason to believe that Teresa's smile as she faced death was any less real than when she was healthier, secure all the while in her family's love. We can see that her drawings were mirrors of her psyche and soma.

Jamie was another child I met in my study of drawings by terminally ill children.

Jamie

These next two pictures, Figures 9 and 10, are from a little girl named Jamie who had an incurable tumor. Dr. Ross had visited Jamie and her mother several times. As you will see these pictures are very colorful.

The first drawing, Figure 9, is a rainbow. With this drawing Jamie had reported that she was "going to make a rainbow." This picture is only one of the two rainbows that Jamie drew during the last few months of her life. The symbolism of the rainbow is revealing information to us from Jamie. Historically, God gave the rainbow to man as a symbol of Peace between Himself and man. It originated with Noah and the Great Flood. After the flood God told Noah that the rainbow would shine to inform man that such a devastating flood would not occur again. It was God's promise of Peace and He was presenting the outward symbol of the rainbow to remind man of this great promise (Gen. 9:13–17). Aside from reminding man, out of God's wisdom it may also have been a reminder to Him as well. So the rainbow and its significant meaning of Peace between God and man is an interesting symbol for a seriously ill child to draw. Because this rainbow takes up the entire page, I wonder if Jamie has thus found Peace with her God.

The next drawing, Figure 10, included four rows of shapes, basically squares and circles. Upon seeing this picture, Dr. Ross informed the mother (as the mother writes):

. . . about the free-floating balloon in the upper-left corner—that Jamie knew she was dying and was without fear. She [Jamie] pictured herself floating off unencumbered into another form of existence.

This was a turning point, for now, as a mother of a dying child, Jamie's mother began to accept her child's impending death.

To add further significance to Jamie's "peace with God," there was another picture (not included here) that contained twenty circles encircling smaller circles. I mention this only for the significance of the circle shape, which is the "balloon shape" Dr. Ross noticed in Figure 10. The circle is a universal symbol; it represents totality, wholeness, fulfillment, the self-contained, and finally God: "God is a circle whose center is everywhere and circumference is nowhere." (Hermes Trismegistus)*

* In J. C. Cooper, *An Illustrated Encyclopaedia of Traditional Symbols* (London: Thames and Hudson, 1978), p. 36.

Combining the significance of the symbols together with information in a letter from Jamie's mother, more understanding comes to us, signifying that Jamie did know and understand her outcome and was at peace.

Jamie's mother writes:

The time for all these drawings is after I learned that there really was nothing left to do for her [Jamie] and that the tumor would run its course. Jamie had not yet begun to lose any functioning. As I mentioned to you, when that did happen, she accepted it much better than I did.

It seems that God and Jamie were at peace with each other. It was Jamie's path. Totality, wholeness, fulfillment had arrived, and it was time for her to travel on. And a mother could begin to accept that, although she would miss her loved one, it truly was her little one's path to follow.

Joann

Leaving the pictures of children, we come to see once again how an adult projects into her drawing a situation of critical importance to her life. We now meet Joann, a forty-nine-year-old mother, who like all others at critical moments in life struggled with questions she sought to answer. When she attended the five-day workshop in which I was teaching, she drew the picture on lined notebook paper shown in Figure 11.

As we shall soon see, this drawing helped her come to grips with a traumatic incident she had experienced. After the workshop, I asked if I might have the drawing and be permitted to use it in my teaching and writing. She was quite willing for me to use the story of her experience with the drawing, but could not part with the original drawing itself. She drew me a "copy" of the picture instead—and I will show and discuss that later—but I was able to get her to agree to send me a color photograph of her original drawing, which is what you see in Figure 11.

The key to the beginning of a healthy process for Joann came about through looking at this picture and deciphering the meaning of its content. This woman was courageous enough to take on the difficult task of understanding and growing in her life's journey, and did not shrug the responsibilities that such growth and learning demand.

For the sake of convenience, and to avoid our missing information in this picture, I have broken the drawing into four equal segments, as shown in Figure 12. I will examine each quadrant, A through D, and then assemble the information in summation to complete the "story" of the picture and of this individual's struggle. I have learned that one projects into a drawing aspects of one's life that are both known and unknown (i.e., not yet developed or conscious). These projections of the known and unknown, or that which is not yet made known, tend to be associated with particular quadrants. I have also learned that it is most productive in studying pictures to begin with the known and work toward the unknown. Thus, I begin in the lower left quadrant and move clockwise toward the lower right quadrant —to the space that represents a very questionable, unknown segment. This movement from known to unknown allows the interpreter to get grounded and be supported while working through a picture's story.

I can recognize what many things in Joann's picture are intended to be, so that I am quickly able to grasp much of its content. In the lower left quadrant, quadrant A, we find a pathway leading to a house. There is also the bottom part of the house and tree trunk, but because the largest part of these objects lies in quadrant B, I will discuss them later. There is grass, so to speak, on each side of this path. It is interesting to find that the pathway is crosshatched. Crosshatching often signifies anxiety.

This causes me to wonder what path is anxiety-provoking to Joann. I take into consideration that this is a path to a house. Could this be Joann's house—her home life? Is it difficult for Joann to deal with the living process within this family? She has a path; obviously she can make her way to the house. This is fortunate for her; however, we still cannot ignore that her way is continually marked with concern.

By now, it should be evident that "reading" a drawing requires paying careful attention to every detail, observing how everything is related or not related, and constantly searching for the possible significance of these data. Positioning, movement, colors, shapes and patterns, the number of objects, and how the picture corresponds to the real world are only a few of the aspects that must be critically examined before impressions can be formulated relative to interpreting the picture's meaning. It is even advisable that a tracing be made of the drawing to ensure that no mark goes unnoticed.

Therefore, continuing to gather each pertinent fact, we proceed to quadrant B, where we notice a house with a door that has a handle. Along the side of the house there are three windows, each with curtains. Below these windows are some green swirls signifying shrubs. The roof is crosshatched and has a chimney, possibly puffing out smoke. On the other hand, the marking above the chimney could be rain, or else it may be that the sky contains both rain and chimney smoke. On the left side of the page, a tree can be seen, leaning to the right. The tree has foliage but does not seem to be entirely secure in its roots. This detailed description is informative, but we now need to scrutinize the drawing for personal meaning.

The first item to draw my attention is the house. It is crosshatched, the same as the pathway and roof. This is further evidence that the home life may be cause for Joann to experience anxiety. Additionally, there are some remarkable attributes of this house. The first is the very small door. If this house is the home of the five individuals on the right, or a house for them to visit, they cannot enter easily through this door. Its height is only 1.2 centimeters, while the adult figures are 2 centimeters and 2.1 centimeters high. Even the smallest figure in quadrant C (1 centimeter high) will encounter some difficulty in passing under the archway of this door. Relating this information to some previous observations made, I then ascertain that the drawing reflects a stressful home life where one may not easily be able to enter. On the other hand, maybe the opposite is true, i.e., that there may be an anxious home life from which one cannot get away. I cannot know at this point, so hold on to the possible finding and continue my intent *examination*.

The second very noticeable attribute of this house is that it has no windows on the front. How unusual! There is not even a small window in the door. Many houses, if not most, have windows in front. Let us consider the use of windows. Windows allow light to come in and make it possible for one to view outside, while substantial protection from the elements is maintained. Windows may also make it possible for one on the outside to see what is on the inside. This personal picture of Joann's makes me wonder if she does not want anyone to see into her home life, and likewise, does not want to face something on the outside that may come to the home. It appears that most of all she wants strong protection—evidenced by the solidness of the front of this house.

I am reminded also that glass can symbolize the spirit. Could it be that Joann has lost her "spirit" in life? Does she doubt God or have no need for Him at this time in her life? Does she wish to cut God out of direct contact in her ilfe and assign Him only to the side, so to speak, if needed? More importantly, where does Joann believe in herself?

Adding to my memory all the data thus far gathered and the questions they have raised, I take note of the third very remark-

FIGURE 1   *Beginnings of Peace*

LAURA

FIGURE 2

FIGURE 3   *Bubbles*

BILL

FIGURE 4   *Wallpaper*

FIGURE 5   *Triangles*

FIGURE 6   *Smiling Girl with Heaven and Earth*

TERESA

FIGURE 7 *Smiling Girl Picking Flowers*

FIGURE 8 *Smiling Girl*

FIGURE 9 *Rainbow*

JAMIE

FIGURE 10 *Shapes*

FIGURE 11   *House with Birds and People*

JOANN

FIGURE 12

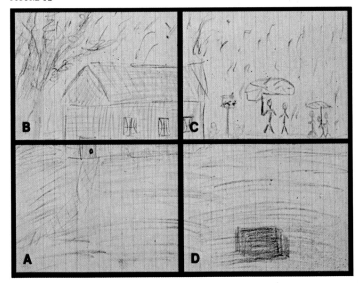

FIGURE 13   Sketch of *House with Birds and People*

JOANN (Cont.)

able attribute of this house. If careful notice is taken, it can be seen that the corner axis between the front and right side of the house does not exist. The house is in danger without this support. I wonder what is going on within Joann if she cannot have support between what is "up front" and what is "at the side."

The questionable smoke at the chimney, together with the rain in the sky, is still perplexing. But I will return to this later.

Moving toward quadrant C, I see a birdhouse with four birds —two red, one blue, and one black bird. Two birds seem to be feeding; the others are either in flight or leaving the feeding area. The bird may be a symbol of the soul. Seeing here that the birds have either been fed, are coming to feed, or else are in the process of feeding, we find that this observation suggests a reassuring position for the indivdual. Food is available for the soul even in the midst of a rainstorm. Thus, I can feel encouraged that Joann is in a very healing, growing position within herself.

Now we look at the rain that enters both quadrant B and quadrant C. Rain could represent purification or cleansing. Of what does Joann need to be cleansed? Why does she need to be purified? Notice that we have purple rain. Purple can represent what is spiritual or perhaps even possessive or possessing. Does Joann need more belief in spiritual possessiveness—with the goal being: God's will be done? What has happened to her to produce so much anxiety that she must shelter herself and prevent anyone from coming into her personal house, i.e., herself? What is her fear that prevents her from letting others see into her while also prohibiting her from looking outside herself (see no front windows)? And how alarming to realize that, between her enlightened side and the defensive front she lives behind, she can find no support for herself. She is obviously hurt from a traumatic incident and feels no certainty of what to do, what to look for, or where to go.

The chimney may be giving off smoke, indicative of a fire

burning within the house. Fire and smoke, appearing either singularly or in combination, oftentimes indicate the need for love and warmth. Adding this possible need to the cleansing need suggested by the rain presents the prospect of a difficult situation for Joann. She needs love and acceptance; but her picture also shows she must renew herself to allow for love to enter her life. I have often found that in order for people to renew themselves, which calls for forgiving themselves, they need first to understand the trauma or event that led to the problem area. After this understanding is accomplished, they need to develop compassion for the person in themselves who got so hurt. C.G. Jung said:

You cannot apply kindness and understanding to others if you have not applied it to yourself. This is quite serious. We are never sufficient to ourselves. This is the burden that everybody has to carry: to live the life we have got to live. So be kind to the least of your sisters who is yourself.

C. G. Jung to Mrs. C., September 24, 1959, *Letters II*.

So at this point I am concerned for Joann, hoping she can forgive herself through understanding what may have happened to her that she now carries as a burden.

In quadrant C we find some additional, important clues. There are individuals in two groupings, both groups walking toward the house or away from it. The fact that these people are drawn as stick figures accounts for our inability to discern much about them, including the direction they are facing. An individual who draws stick figures is often uncomfortable about revealing, either to himself or to others, his authentic self.

Joann tells me that the larger umbrella is held by her husband and that she is walking beside him; the three children are together under the other umbrella. What is so very unusual about Joann and her husband is their position under the umbrella. I suggest we "climb into the picture" to become the man carrying the umbrella and then to become the woman. In the man's position, we realize that the umbrella is held in the hand farthest away from his wife. This provides her with only the barest amount of protection. We also notice that the umbrella had to be drawn with an added extension to be able to reach over Joann's head at all. Perhaps Joann realizes that her husband is not including her under his "umbrella" and her drawing expresses her need to have this umbrella extended to include herself. Moreover, as we become the woman in the drawing, we wonder why she does not stand closer to her husband. Anyone, having experienced sharing an umbrella with somebody else, knows that the umbrella needs to be held between them in order to provide the best protection and that it further helps to huddle together with arms around each other's waist. Noticing the distance between Joann and her husband in this picture, I am led to question the marital relationship and what may have occurred in the anxious home life of these two adults.

The children are by themselves and appear to be more secure under their umbrella. We need to know the ages of the children; they appear to be young—perhaps between nine and twelve years of age. However, Joann informs me that they are adults in their twenties! These are the figures of her son, daughter, and son-in-law, and they are out walking with Joann and her husband. I wonder why Joann must keep these adults so childlike and under so much protection. Why can she not allow them to become adults? Since she has drawn them so much smaller than she and her husband, what does this say about her relationship and attitude toward them? When I asked whether she treated them as though they were children, she told me a very moving story.

Her oldest son is buried in the box in quadrant D. He had

been murdered at work on a Friday evening, with no apparent cause for the crime. Tragically, his body was not discovered until the next day. Joann told me, "In my son's wallet we found Paul Cotton's song 'Bad Weather' written on a piece of paper: 'And I believe it is going to rain.'" And this drawing is of a rainy day, although Joann surprised herself when she made this correlation a few weeks after the picture was drawn.

This tragedy caused Joann to take special care of her remaining children. She phoned her married daughter regularly to see if she and her husband were safely home in the evening. Her younger son, who still lived at home, was constantly being checked. As a mother, Joann feared for her remaining children's lives, and thought that her protection was needed. But this kind of mothering had become unbearable to her children, and they were beginning to draw away from her. Her husband was also pulling away, alienated by her inappropriate behavior stemming from her unresolved feelings about her son's murder.

While discussing this picture's content and working on understanding its meaning, Joann readily admitted her sense of overprotection and the noticeable withdrawal of her children. Not only was she able to understand their response, but she was willing to accept responsibility for triggering it. Joann was beginning to be more conscious of her actions and their ramifications. She wanted to alter her behavior.

What happened to Joann the mother and to Joann the woman is deep in her psyche and older than the days she has lived on this earth. Her life as a woman was reactivated toward the role of the nurturing mother and protector by the tragic death of her son. When a mother loses a child, this Great Mother archetype may manifest itself regardless of the age of the child at the time of his death. Joann needs to understand this natural tendency and to have compassion for her instinctive, nurturing mother drive. She can then begin dealing with the person inside herself who wants to be overprotective, but in the process stifles her relationship with her remaining children. She can also begin to come to grips with the fact that regardless of all she was able to do for her son, there was nothing she could do that would have prevented his murder. As I spoke with Joann, I realized she was a very courageous woman and wanted to deal with these issues in order to get on with her life, to improve her relationship with her family, as well as to foster growth in her marriage.

We talked briefly about many facets of her life, considering what she was doing and could do to bring about this change that she desired. Two days later, our group workshop ended, and as I was preparing to leave the workshop site, I met Joann by chance in the foyer of our meeting hall. I had an opportunity to converse with her for a while, and it was at that time that I requested her drawing as an example of the usefulness of studying a drawing to bring into consciousness some unprocessed concern. She replied, quite naturally, that she could not part with this picture. Then I asked whether she might be able to sketch a duplicate for me, explaining that a quick, simple sketch would do to serve my memory, and that from this copy I could help others to grasp its content. Figure 13 shows the sketch Joann did for me.

We had no colored pencils handy; only a ball-point pen was available. Joann had her original drawing next to her as she sketched the copy for me. When we compare Figures 11 and 13 we can observe the significant differences. In the second drawing the children are taller and the doorway to the house is arched and more accessible than what we see in the original drawing. These alterations are promising signs for growth and change. The second drawing contains less crosshatching than the first, yet the pathway is still tenuous. Most importantly, Joann left the dead son out of the family portrait, suggesting that she is accepting reality and resolving her guilt and grief. Joann's husband now has a phallic projection between his legs. I realize that Joann still has many personal issues in addition to those within the family to deal with, but this is indeed a very encouraging picture concerning this woman's inner growth.

As we were leaving, Joann mentioned that she was planning to invite her son, daughter, and son-in-law for dinner on the weekend. She was eager to tell them that she realized what she had been doing but was attempting now to recognize them as adults. She wanted to tell her husband that she loved him and that she knew she needed to cope constructively with their son's death. I saw this as a very positive outcome.

A few years later, I heard that Joann was doing work on the national level for parents who have lost their loved ones through trauma. From Joann's account, and from what I have heard from friends, Joann has dealt with her loss and has regained strength to find meaning in what she has encountered in her life. I believe that her drawing brought to consciousness issues that needed to be processed in order to heal her psychological wounds. This healing was necessary before her psychic energy could be free to function creatively for her.

Empirical studies on the use of drawings as an aid in diagnosis and treatment indicate that extemporaneous drawings reflect both psychological and somatic processes, as we have seen to some extent in the preceding examples. A patient may not be able to reveal verbally his urgent desires and needs or his past, present, or potential condition; but these important features may be reflected through the symbolic language of drawings. This symbolic language, which begins at the unconscious level, functions both in drawings and in dreams. It serves to help the individual maintain harmony and balance in his life. When the symbolic language of dreams or drawings remains at the unconscious level, its efficiency in correcting certain conditions is reduced. When an individual can be helped to bring into consciousness and assimilate what his symbolic language is trying to teach him, he can immediately begin to work toward needed changes in his life that otherwise might come about only after many months of indirect movement toward improvement. In the case of a child, the cooperation of certain adults may be needed to bring about the necessary change.

This chapter would not be complete without mention of the dangers involved in attempting to analyze extemporaneous drawings. To the layman, this work may look fairly simple, and one may even attempt to interpret his children's drawings or drawings from friends. But drawing analysis should not be treated as a parlor game. It is a very serious undertaking to counsel an individual, using as a tool the reflections from the person's unconscious realm. It is a delicate task to help a person grasp what is just at the threshold of consciousness, whether it involves facing death or preparing for a renewed life.

Interpreting pictures is quite difficult without reading into them what one already knows or suspects to be there. For this reason, it is recommended that the individual's full case history not be examined until *after* the drawing has been evaluated. Another pitfall occurs when the interpreter projects his own unconscious material into the person's drawing. The only way to avoid this is for the interpreter to undergo his own personal analysis first. Therefore, in order to analyze drawings properly, one must not only have the necessary professional training, but must obtain personal preparation as well.

In this chapter we have studied the drawings from two adults and three children in an attempt to understand the usefulness of such drawings at significant times in one's life. From Laura we have learned how she unconsciously reflected into her drawing deficiencies, concerning her psychological development, that needed to be compensated for in order that she become a more whole person. Furthermore, Laura's picture made us aware of an inner knowledge of one's potential destiny, in reference to a somatic condition, where the pictorial evidence precedes the clinical diagnosis. Bill taught us the importance of healing the spirit even when we cannot heal the body. Teresa's drawings demonstrated for us how a child's physical prognosis can be forecasted by the child's preconscious knowledge, just as we saw with Laura; and also, how the psyche responds to somatic developments. Jamie's picture showed us how parents can be helped to come to grips with their child's death. From Joann we learned how the drawing-analysis experience can help one to heal old wounds, renew oneself, and move toward restoring harmony in one's life and home. We have learned that understanding pictorial language can help open the door to wholeness.

III

PARENT CARE: TOTAL INVOLVEMENT IN THE CARE OF A DYING CHILD

BY MARTHA PEARSE ELLIOTT

I THOUGHT that it would be worse than it was. I thought that losing a child to leukemia was the ultimate in tragedy.

The loss and the tragedy cannot be denied. And the nineteen months between diagnosis and death certainly weren't easy. But they weren't as hard as I thought they would be.

Meredith was six when she died in January 1973, in a Houston hospital six hundred miles from our Kansas home. It had been a long time since we first walked through those doors in the dark of night, afraid and alone, in a strange place.

But the people, the doctors, the institution that shaped our lives during that time gave us the perspective that made her death more acceptable than it might have been in another setting.

Thanatology, the study of death and dying, is a fashionable topic today, with researchers such as Elisabeth Kübler-Ross helping society to cast off some of its taboos about the dying.

Personal experience taught me and my family many of the same concepts discovered through detailed research. Among these are that death is not necessarily totally negative, and that each of us, whether we are dying ourselves or comforting someone else who is dying, has resources to call upon to enrich the time that is left and to accept the end with some modicum of grace.

My own resources were not just the ones I expected. Fortunately, there were some basic essentials: Jerry, my husband; Hunter, my twelve-year-old son; Meredith, the stricken child, who had unusual perception and maturity; and my own ability to function reasonably well under stress.

Three other factors, though, were instrumental in shaping the experience. They were the availability of a parent-care pediatric ward, a hospital subculture of helping mothers, and a supportive and empathetic friend.

The parent-care ward was the most significant. Once I discovered the difference between an ordinary hospital situation and a specialized center that emphasizes full parent involvement as well as aggressive medical care, I was willing to take extraordinary measures to be a part of the latter.

Parent-care pediatric units are few and far between, mostly at medical centers that specialize in catastrophic diseases of children. Obviously, few hospitals are geared toward long-term care, so extensive parent involvement is not practical.

But many care centers do exist where parents could be more involved then they are. The arguments for keeping parents out of the picture are many. Physicians feel parents are better off not knowing everything, nurses feel parents are in the way and do more harm than good, administrators may feel the extra cost of maintaining facilities for parents is not only unjustifiable but akin to running a hotel—there are many other logical reasons why traditional care should prevail. Logical, but not necessarily helpful.

Parent care is not altogether efficient. It involves risks, personal conflicts, and bothersome routines that medical personnel easily could live without. But in a well-managed unit, parents actually relieve the staff of many duties that in turn reduce the cost of extra salaries.

More importantly, parent care often gives the parents and the child a deeply meaningful experience, one that provides the family with a sense of helpfulness in doing all that is possible. The experience also helps the entire family to understand what the child's illness and treatment entail and how to cope with the daily strains, as well as the possibility of the child's eventual death.

Needless to say, the staff in such a situation must be extraordinary. In our own situation, when there often were as many as thirty families on the floor, living together in crowded conditions, all of whom had children with some form of malignancy, the sheer volume of work and activity in that environment was often overwhelming. The floor always was in high gear.

Also, in a situation in which families live on the ward for extended periods of time, from days to months, the staff eventually knows the family well and sometimes makes strong attachments to the children and their parents. That all of these children might, and often do, die is a strain that most ordinary hospital personnel do not have to face.

Yet, at this hospital, when death is near, the curtains are not necessarily drawn nor the doors closed. Staff attention, if anything, is heightened. Previous professional/patient barriers are dropped and new warmths established.

But staff cannot fill all needs. Though all the medical personnel we met were informative, open, honest, and helpful in every respect, they could not meet all of the personal needs of each family. So the families turned to each other. And "other parents" constituted the second most helpful resource.

This support is true not only to my own experience, but is upheld in the psychological literature. Parents teach each other, lean on each other in time of need, share experiences, or perhaps just babysit.

It is a family, a subculture of its own, with rules and limits. Rule number one is that one never turns one's back on someone in need.

Our own first night at the hospital is an example. Meredith had been diagnosed and referred to Houston rather hurriedly. We caught the first plane, then foolishly tried to drive from the airport to the hospital, thirty miles away. It was dark, and in no time I was lost in the spaghetti-maze of freeway. Two hours and many frustrating miles later we pulled into the medical center parking lot. The sign on the spotlighted pink marble building in front of me spelled out the words that so frightened me. Tumor Institute.

Then came the associations I had previously blocked out. Tumor, cancer, leukemia, death. So this is a cancer hospital. They sent her here to die. And they didn't even tell us.

I was frightened, frustrated, disappointed. And I didn't dare reveal to Meredith just how dramatic the situation really was. Above all, maintain a calm exterior, I thought, no matter what was going on inside.

On the pediatrics floor a bed was waiting, and the admitting routine went quite smoothly. After things settled down and Meredith went to sleep, I prepared to spend the rest of the night on a chair in the lounge, then find a motel the next day.

Two cheery mothers were waiting for me. I could not believe how anyone who spent five minutes on that floor possibly could be sane, much less be having such a good time. It was like a dorm for unwed mothers. The kids were asleep and the moms were sitting around in bathrobes and curlers, just having a wonderful time.

The two mothers made me comfortable, and then began to tell me about this strange place.

First, I wasn't going to any motel. Mothers stayed at the hospital. Sometimes fathers, too, but not usually. A cot was provided for each mother next to her child's bed. They showed me where food, linens, and supplies were kept and how I was to make use of them. One mother even made my bed.

They told me about the routine, the doctors, what, in general, the hospital expected of me, and what I could expect from them. The nurses told me much the same thing the next day, but it was more meaningful coming from those women in my own situation.

Later, during the ofttimes lengthy periods of hospitalization, we mothers leaned upon each other a great deal. In the daytime we hustled the kids through procedures, routines, and school-work. At night we huddled in corners and talked about our children, our families, our fears and frustrations, our angers, joys, and despair. We needed each other.

And when a mother left after the death of her child, many of us felt a selfish sort of loss, not like the simple philosophy of one child I knew who would say when one of her little friends would die, "Well, that's one we don't have to worry about anymore."

The mechanics of our own particular form of parent care, briefly overviewed, were simple. The primary involvement was medical. The first few days were spent in extensive testing and diagnosis. Every procedure and every result was explained to us, and to our child.

At diagnosis there was a conference with the chief of pediatrics, who discussed with us every facet of the disease, the drugs, the degree to which we could participate in care, current research and treatment success of leukemia and other malignant diseases.

In short, he laid it all on the line, answered every probing question Jerry and I had, and even gave us extra reading material to help quench our thirst for knowledge.

We were like most parents. We had an insatiable need for information, but none of us was really able to compute it all at first. We forgot much of what we were told, and had to be told again, and sometimes again. The need for an explanation, plus the sheer volume of information, plus the denial working in all of us, really kept full comprehension far from the realm of realistic expectation at this early stage.

The secondary involvement was more practical. Life on the pediatrics floor sometimes stretched into weeks and months, while doctors tried to induce a remission. We spent the entire summer of 1971 in Houston, most of it in the hospital.

The daily routine was just that. Routine. The children were kept busy with treatments, schoolwork, occupational therapy projects, or in play with parents or other children.

Mothers busied themselves in menial tasks they otherwise might have found boring. We were not required to do any of them, but we were allowed to, and most of us chose to.

Of course, there was the constant task of keeping our little six-by-ten-foot corner of the room in some semblance of order. No small job considering the ratio of accumulated paraphernalia to allotted space. Every task—eating, sleeping, playing, treatment—required total rearrangement of furnishings.

We changed sheets, carried food trays, took temperatures, in some cases helped administer drugs, "assisted" at all routine medical procedures, including frequent bone marrows and spinal taps. We gave blood and platelets.

We learned to regulate IVs. We learned the drugs and their dosages, and we watched like hawks to make sure each child got his proper treatment.

The supply closet was open, and we helped ourselves. When the children were out-patients, a typical mother's purse might contain: Band-Aids, tape, gauze dressings, alcohol pads, an emesis pan, perhaps a few syringes, saline and heparin solutions, drugs, a bar of antibacterial soap or at least a handfull of Wash'n'Dries, and assorted other medical oddities. We all were equipped like junkies.

We learned blood counts and their meanings. This was especially important for out-patients, who had to know exactly how vulnerable they might be to infection. Was the white count high enough to go to school, or the movie? With blood counts three times a week at home in Kansas, we would not wait for doctors to finish their long working days, call the lab, call us back, explain what it meant, etc., etc. The doctors soon learned to authorize the labs to give us the information, and we could figure it out for ourselves.

We learned to administer some of the drugs in out-patient care, too. For example, some drugs were given three times a day, IV, at regular intervals. It was impractical to drive across town for injections at seven, three, and eleven o'clock daily for two weeks or more, with no guarantee that the emergency room would be able to administer the drug on time.

So we learned to do it ourselves. The doctors implanted an IV needle and secured it with an armboard and heparin lock. Three times a day we mixed fresh drugs at home, tested the IVs to see if they were working (if they weren't, it entailed a trip to the hospital after all), and gave the drugs or even let the child do it. Then off to play, or school, or back to bed, with a minimum of disruption and stress.

Parents also learned when to panic and when not to panic. Gradually they learned that in some cases they must expect vomiting, elevated temperatures, or pains in strange places. They also learned that perhaps a headache or a bruise or a gain in weight might be a serious matter.

We were, in many ways, the doctors' assistants. We had minimum knowledge and skills, but enough to report on many things the staff could not possibly be expected to observe. And while informed parents make many mistakes, uninformed ones may make a lot more. In addition, the uninformed wallow in uncertainty, insecurity, and constant apprehension. Ignorance is not necessarily bliss.

The important thing is that, although parent care is not a perfect approach, almost every parent I have ever met in this kind of situation appreciated the opportunity to help with any task, however unpleasant, boring, or even frightening. It is not always joyous, but it has its rewards.

I know of no parent who really enjoyed cleaning up vomit or changing a smelly dressing. But I know few who preferred that someone else do it.

Any help that a parent can provide gives him or her a feeling of worth and helpfulness in an otherwise helpless situation. I know a professional woman who recalled her mother's death from a malignancy some years ago, and said how she told the nurses she would gladly scrub the floors if it would free someone to give her mother some aid and comfort in her dying moments. The kind of aid she herself was medically unable to give.

Parents helped each other, too. The best advice I ever got came from two other mothers. One, an early acquaintance at the hospital, had a child that frankly disturbed me. She was the essence of death, a virtual skeleton. Every unpleasantness that can happen to a cancer patient had happened to this child. And I did not like her.

Of course, I never really knew her, although we shared a room for a time. But she was an agonizing reminder of what might happen to my beautiful little girl, and I was very uncomfortable around her. Later, she and all she symbolized haunted me in my dreams.

Her mother and I were never close. We never really had the time, for M. died shortly after we arrived at the hospital. But I learned much from listening, in those mothers-only lines waiting for the shower every night, where the conversations sometimes got close and heavy.

The morning M. died, we somehow missed the news. As her

mother was leaving the hospital for the last time, she came into our room, took my hands in hers, and said, "Good luck to you."

Instantly I knew, and I was afraid. M. was the first. So kids really did die here.

We stepped into the hall, and she said, "Don't be afraid to let her go." We embraced, and she went away, leaving me with that simple but weighty philosophy. And it was an invaluable legacy.

Another helpful mother was an early roommate who was responsible for teaching me most of the hospital rules of survival, and who still remains a close friend.

It was her son's death, more than a year before Meredith's, that first forced us to confront Meredith with the death of a friend who had the same disease she had.

We visited the family many times in their home, where Meredith saw how the parents openly, but not melodramatically, dealt with their loss, and how they resumed a happy life with their remaining children without apparent ill feeling toward the sick child or the hospital situation that had separated them for so long.

It was this woman who gently suggested we make advance arrangements for the funeral, autopsy, and all the things that must be done in case of death.

It was she who told me, after she herself had been through an inordinately long and difficult struggle, that "it isn't as bad as you think it's going to be." And it wasn't.

These two factors, the planned program of parent care and the spontaneous helping-mother subculture, were the most helpful elements in the process of coping with the death of our child.

But there were other significant persons, one of whom contributed some of the interviews that follow. In retrospect I see this as another common pattern. Most parents rely on some "significant other" in addition to the immediate family or the other mothers. It may be a friend or relative, but I have noticed the amazing frequency with which these strong attachments are made with other staff members.

It is not usually a doctor involved on the case, but frequently it is a staff member from some other department that may have frequent contact with the family. Secretaries, physical or occupational therapists, lab technicians, nurses or doctors from other departments, and many others. Every child seems to have a "special" friend on the staff.

Meredith's special friend was a young psychology graduate student doing research at the hospital during the summer of 1971. N.'s patients were mostly children with solid tumors who were receiving rehabilitation therapy. Thus, we were not on her "list." But our roommates were, and in that group setting she and Meredith soon developed a fascinating rapport.

At the end of the summer, N. returned to the University of Texas, and Meredith returned home after achieving a long-awaited remission. Before we all parted ways, this young woman confided to me that she was a cancer patient herself, with a new (second) and inoperable tumor. I was cautioned not to mention it to Meredith—ever.

Within a month N. called long-distance to ask if she could visit us for a weekend. I reluctantly said yes. I resented her request for many reasons, but Meredith had developed such an attachment for her that I couldn't really refuse.

The visit was a near disaster. Some of its events are detailed in "The Team" interview that follows. But for all its pain, it was the beginning of an intense relationship among the three of us. Later we all faced death together.

Meredith maintained a remission for a year after her initial hospitalization. During that time we made frequent out-patient trips to Houston, where we often saw N. without her white uniform and in the new patient role. Her family offered us a place to stay. We accepted, and we saw them often.

During that year Meredith did well and lived a relatively normal life. N. got sicker and sicker. Three times I said good-bye, convinced she would not survive the next treatment or next surgery. She not only survived but is seemingly cancer-free today. A rare success story considering the extraordinary obstacles she had to overcome.

And I survived. I had hidden for many months the symptoms that told almost at the time Meredith first became ill, that I had multiple sclerosis. Until I couldn't hide them any longer.

Today it is hard to conceptualize my death from anything. I have no noticeable disability and I feel too good to think about dying. But in the spring of 1972, when I gave up trying to fool myself and the world around me that I was a superwoman, death became a real threat, albeit an unrealistic one at that time. My only goal then was to be strong enough to see Meredith through her ordeal. I got a lot more than that.

For all my fears, my disease did not ever interfere with my ability to function normally or to care for my child. And in many ways it became a source of strength and special empathy in our relationship.

In late August of 1972, Meredith relapsed, coincidentally after an impressive visit to a new children's hospital in another state where several of our favorite Texas doctors and personnel had gone. "Which" hospital became a real conflict. We chose Texas.

Five difficult months followed between the first relapse and her death in January. Only two months were spent in the hospital, three weeks at home and the rest as an out-patient. Each full day was spent in clinic. "Home" was with N.'s family or at the apartment we shared with other Wichita families who had children in treatment at Houston.

A change in personnel in pediatrics had left a change in the mood of the floor. Or perhaps those of us "old-timers" had overreacted to the changes because there was something about coming back in a relapse that had ominous overtones. The first time we came, there was no way to go (almost) but up. This time we knew it would be downhill all the way.

A roller-coaster of relapse, remission, relapse, remission carried us through the fall. A bout with pneumonia after Thanksgiving plus a new drug therapy left Meredith more vulnerable than ever to infection. Christmas was approaching, and things were looking dimmer.

Two weeks before Christmas we bought a tiny tree and spent the next few days decorating it. I strung popcorn and cranberries, and Meredith made and cut out Santas and stars and angels. That scruffy little tree became a symbol of the last hope, the last effort. It truly was the prettiest tree we ever had. The little string of lights shone like a beacon in our apartment window.

Four days before Christmas the bone marrow report was bad—again. I wasn't surprised, but Meredith was crestfallen. She was "due" for remission. During the entire fall she had been taking the bad bone marrows in stride, because she knew the next one would be all right, even if just for a short time. She cried hard. It was the beginning of the end.

The doctors sent us home. But we couldn't go home—Hunter was very sick, and we couldn't risk exposing Meredith to the infection. So we struggled with our decision of what to do. It was the last Christmas, we all knew, and it was going to be a good one, no matter what.

We almost stayed in Houston. Our "family" on the pediatrics floor was still there and we had become so close that it would have been comfortable to stay with them. Even the ones who were liberated for Christmas Day brought turkey and trimmings and champagne—and the rest of their families—back to the hospital for a swinging Christmas feast.

But we decided to start driving anyway, winding our way back home the long way, through Missouri to attend a family reunion Christmas Eve at my parents' home. Our little tree went with us. It was a happy time, despite our disappointments, and Hunter even got well the same day. We headed home. As we turned westward, I thought this must be like Dorothy and the Wizard of Oz. All we want is to go home to Kansas.

We pulled into our own driveway at 9:30 P.M. Christmas Eve, one step ahead of Santa. Friends had swathed the house in crisp-smelling greenery and red candles and bowls of fruit and nuts. The fire was blazing. The tree was decorated and presents were piled around it. The family was together again, and despite the ravages of disease and stress and separation, it was the finest Christmas we ever had.

The following week, though, was not so enjoyable. Meredith needed several transfusions. Her blood counts were poor. She began to be openly afraid of dying. "Can you die if you don't have any polys?" she would ask. "No," I answered, and explained why. "But I'm so scared," she said.

I tried to assure her that although these things seemed frightening, she had gone through them all before and counts always came back up. But she saw right through me. That week we made funeral arrangements.

In a few days an infection stirred, and we were on our way back to Texas. It was soon overcome, but an emotional change had taken place in both of us. I can see it clearly now, but at the time I only knew that something was different, something indefinable.

We both began to withdraw. We would snuggle together on my cot and were perfectly content to see or talk to no one else, not even our roommates, whom we were so fond of. Meredith would talk of being afraid. "Afraid of what?" I asked. "Just afraid," she would say.

The therapy situation worried me, and I pressed for a medical conference. I was apprised of what I already knew. Things were not going well, but there were still drugs we could try. With options still left, things were looking up again.

A week later Meredith was better and got a weekend pass. Jerry and Hunter flew down, and we headed for our apartment for what we hoped would be a quiet weekend together. We arrived to find strangers had moved in, thrown all our things into the hall, and the place was strewn with cigarette butts and rotting food. The stench was overpowering. We couldn't find the culprits, and our only choice was to go to a motel.

We never did solve the mystery, although we tried all weekend. Anger and phone bills rose in direct proportion. But by Sunday it didn't matter because another kind of disaster struck. Meredith complained of symptoms we both recognized as pneumonia.

She was in a great deal of pain. We calmly gathered our belongings and headed back toward the hospital.

Jerry and Hunter flew home that night. As the week wore on, Meredith's blood counts got lower and lower while the pneumonia took a stronger hold. By Friday we knew she desperately needed infection-fighting white cells. Fortunately, we were at one of the few hospitals in the country that have leukapheresis —white-cell extraction—machines. Jerry flew down to give the precious cells, as her preferred donor.

Leukapheresis is a thoroughly miserable way to be of help. Donors are made ill to force the body to produce enough white cells to extract. Without them, many patients would die needlessly. But donors are true heroes.

Jerry couldn't get on the machine for several days. Meanwhile, Meredith was put on the critical list and we began to prepare for the inevitable. My father, a physician in Missouri, came to be with us. And after making one of the most difficult decisions of the entire course of Meredith's disease, we called for Hunter to fly down.

We had tried to prepare Hunter for Meredith's death as much as possible, but he had always had a difficult time with it. He had told us at Christmas, after we had confronted him with the possibility of an earlier death than we had expected, that he did not want to come to Houston to see her if she "got bad."

We made him come anyway. It was painful for all of us. But once he actually saw her, even though she was in a coma, he really responded to her. He stroked her head, told her who he was and that he loved her. In effect, he told her good-bye.

He was not at the hospital when she actually died, and he asked on the way home if there were any possibility that they made a mistake, that she wasn't really dead. At first I thought that was a very immature question for a twelve-year-old. After all, he was old enough to know dead is dead. And then I remembered asking the same question the first time I faced the death of a young friend. I was fourteen at the time.

Facing that final reality was difficult. Even for me. I had known better than anyone in the family that death was catching up with her, day by day. I grieved along the way, especially at the diagnosis and again at the first relapse. (A doctor once told us that the first relapse is the cruelest blow of all.)

And when the end came, we were ready. None of us wanted it to go on. We just wanted it to be over. I watched her take her last breath. And though I cried once more, I was relieved that she didn't hurt anymore. And she looked pink and healthy and at peace.

Somehow it wasn't the same for any of us when we saw her three days later in the casket. It was a different kind of dead. She was really finally, thoroughly dead. I had questioned the mortician earlier about why we had to go through all this business of having her dressed and coming to see her when we planned to have the casket closed at the services. We had already seen her dead. He just said we had to. And now I know why. It was a finality none of us anticipated.

And since then, I have had difficulties with my sense of loss, I have had trouble readjusting to my family after we learned to live without each other for so long, and I have had trouble finding direction and purpose in life because my values have changed and the old ones are no longer adequate. But I have not had any trouble accepting the reality of Meredith's death. It was the "realest" thing that ever happened.

My feelings about my daughter and her struggle with death are not unique. Nor are they universal. My hope is that much helpful information will come from current research in the area of death and dying. And that we will all be delivered from our death fears and taboos, so that we may be free to live fuller and more satisfying lives. Even those, perhaps especially those, who are seriously ill and dying. Until recently the trail was uncharted.

In the material that follows, there are glimpses of life and death on a children's cancer ward. Some is more of my own experience and observation of parents' feelings about their childrens' diseases, effects on the family, values, life-styles.

The conversations were taped six weeks after Meredith's death, when I visited several friends who have worked at the hospital—our young psychologist/patient/friend, and another staff member with experience and training in one of the helping professions. The conversations are quite personal in nature and are offered as experience and, I hope, insight. They are not to be construed as scientifically controlled conclusions or any reflection of hospital policy. Names, except those of my own family, are fictitious.

Family Stress

In many cases, when a catastrophic illness strikes a family, an unexpected side effect may be divorce. Accurate statistics are not readily available, but professionals in several different hospital situations of this type have estimated the divorce rate during the child's illness to be four to five times the average. There is no way to document the divorce rate after the child's death in most cases.

MOTHER: We were talking about how you handle families in trouble. You know, whether families do recover if they start out in trouble.

COUNSELOR: Obviously, there are a certain number of families who are in trouble before they come in, that may have been in trouble all the way along. And these families, in my experience, pretty quickly break up. And then you have a number of other families who probably would have gone along okay—not what you and I could consider satisfactory marriages, but the kind of relationships most people have, without ever realizing their potentialities, but without really splitting—that are tremendously strained. And these people quite frequently do break up either somewhere along in the treatment process of the child, or after the death of the child. And a number of these people I would estimate would not break up if this or some other severe crisis did not occur.

There are certain other marriages that I feel are considerably strengthened. That doesn't mean they don't have their bad times in the process, but I think if people can make this whole experience of having to suffer and lose a child and endure it, I think they can make something positive come of it for a marriage, just as you know individuals can.

One of the real difficulties here as far as doing any marital counseling is, so often there is only one partner here. And I don't mean you can't do considerably with one person, but just as any kind of therapy, if one person is in therapy and the other is not, that in itself may contribute to a marriage breakup. So what we try to do, if someone here indicates they want to be worked with and there's no way we can work with both of them, is to encourage the other person to get help wherever they are. And then we do as much as we can here.

One couple from here in Texas . . . I got them to go to a family service agency there, and they went a time or two, and as many people do, when the immediate crisis had passed they dropped out. But they periodically came back, and occasionally the mother would call me up long-distance and I kept trying to get them to go back, and pointing out . . . that they really hadn't solved anything. And she had all kinds of physical symptoms, and I told her I thought it was related to what was *not* going on between the two of them. And oh, no, they didn't want anything to do with it. But finally they did, and now they're working regularly. Well, this is the kind of thing that can be done.

A lot of crises people have, if a guy loses his job, or if one or the other is unfaithful, or whatever, things that can shatter marriages, are things people can at least work on together.

And I think one of the things that's concerned me so in the way we treat children here is that we separate families, immediately. Not always, because there is the occasional individual who will move the family here, if the man does the kind of employment where this is possible, and I think this is infinitely more satisfactory. But obviously everybody can't move to Houston.

MOTHER: I think there's another point, too. And I've discussed this with several mothers. We felt like, well, to move to

Houston is to give in to this disease and it will rule my life. That's not to say it doesn't take up 90 percent of your existence anyway, which somehow you can handle, but to say it takes up 100 percent is more than I will admit. I know my first reaction was, well, we'll move to Houston. My next one was, I will *not* do any such thing. But I can see if you live here it's easier. Of course, we had an apartment, which is easier.

COUNSELOR: No, you didn't have a husband and child here.

MOTHER: No, but I had enough friends here that I had "family" and so it was easier.

COUNSELOR: But I'm still talking about the real family, the nuclear family. And I understand what you mean because I'm opposed to what some doctors say, you know to someone who has, say, asthma, say, move to Arizona. Well, hell, if you don't want to move to Arizona that's creating more problems. And I really don't encourage people to move here. All I'm saying is that's the only way I know for people to be geographically together, and I'm aware that people being geographically together doesn't mean that they're together.

But I'm also aware that physical separation, in and of itself, can be pretty devastating for most marriages. You know, because people grow, and if they're not together, they grow apart. There's just no other way to do it. And, you know, my own personal reaction to that, and I can understand that, is that if any of you mothers up there who have a child with leukemia think it doesn't rule your life, you're kidding yourselves. 'Cause it does.

MOTHER: Oh, it does, but here are fine breaking points, where you just have to say, "This is it. . . ."

The separation is difficult. I know at first it brought us very much closer together, but when we got home, after three months down here, everything fell apart, and it's been very difficult since then. You grow in different ways. You have different expectations at different times. Just nothing seems to mesh. But, uh. . . .

COUNSELOR: No, I wish there were some logical way, and of course the way our society is set up with the man traditionally the breadwinner and the woman the child-carer. But I wish there was a logical way to figure out if this is the best way to do it. I certainly understand from the medical treatment that having a center makes sense rather than having everybody in small places trying to treat something that obviously nobody can be as qualified as a center where you have all the technological advantages.

But I wish we could have some way to alternate parents staying with children. Now occasionally this happens. The mother's pregnant, or she gets sick and the father comes and stays with the child, and occasionally a grandparent does this. But this is valuable not only for the relief of the mother, but for the involvement of the father, because I think so many times the barriers that come up, even the disagreement about treatment, are simply because until you're here every day and endure it every day and see what happens, it's very hard for any parent to make an intelligent decision about what they want done. And there are so many other things operating, you know, so much guilt, so much. . . .

The virtues of parent care may be many. One of the most important is that the mother is allowed to stay with the child to provide as much constant care and reassurance as if the child were at home.

But among the unhappy effects of parent care is that fathers sometimes feel left out, and often feel much more strain than the mothers. The more a father is separated from the situation, whether for occupational or geographical reasons, or in cases where the mother may shut him out emotionally, the more a father may feel jealous, threatened, and certainly unprepared for a possible death. The security of the hospital does not necessarily extend beyond mother and child.

The strongest of families are strained. If efforts are made to see that the family as a unit is part of the total experience from the beginning, some of the strains can be ameliorated. It is a cumbersome problem at best.

New methods of rehabilitation of cancer patients, which include the concepts of family problem prevention, are being tried. An adult amputee, for example, may spend the postoperative period in a rehabilitation, rather than general hospitalization, setting. There he learns aids in daily living and management of a prosthesis. Before he is discharged completely he and his family may move to temporary living quarters on the hospital grounds, where the family becomes reacquainted under his new circumstances. It is a psychological and physiological acclimation period, a halfway house, where the security of the hospital is close by, yet the "home" is not a hospital environment.

PSYCHOLOGIST: You can't do away with the anxiety each family goes through, nor the fear, the depression, the frustration, at times despair. These are all universal in dealing with the patients and their families. And some very unique problems with siblings. I think, like Mrs. B., that fathers should be more a part.

MOTHER: You see more fathers on the floor now than last year.

PSYCHOLOGIST: Exactly. Jim's daddy and Carl's and Freddie's.

MOTHER: And Jerry. I told Jerry that as long as Meredith wasn't in the hospital, it wasn't that necessary that he fly down. But when she was, it was the greatest thing he could have done. Of course he was here a lot that first summer when Meredith first got sick. But the only other father on the floor that summer was Tom's daddy, and he lived here in town. Now Crissy's daddy comes in every weekend. And Annie's when he can, or when a decision has to be made.

PSYCHOLOGIST: So you have the fathers coming in on the weekends. I think it makes it easier for the men to understand if they come in, but I don't really think the weekend is a very good time because the hospital kind of closes up then. The guys who stay during the week see what really goes on. The humdrum, the waiting. The kids don't have to go for treatment on the weekend. The fathers see it relatively quiet. They don't have to tear their hair out during the week trying to get from one place to the next while the nurses are doing this and that and cultures are being taken. If the child dies, being part of it makes it that much easier for him to accept.

MOTHER: Jack has had some difficulty accepting this. When his wife came in yesterday, she said this is it, it's all over. And he wasn't ready to hear that. Now you see intelligent people who are there a lot, like Jack, who are that close and watch it all, and all of a sudden he said he doesn't believe it. So . . . Dr. C. came in this morning and explained it to him, everything that was happening. Now Mary told him the same thing, but it had to come from Dr. C. because she's the doctor. And I don't know why that had to be. Other daddies had the same problem. In a sense Jerry had the same problem.

Sometimes you can just take so much of this crap and you have to say . . . and I'm speaking strictly from a frustrated mother's point of view, one who's been through this for a long period of time, and I'm sorry it's this way. It's the end of many families. You can just take so much of this enduring, no end to it, no good end to it, no definite end to it in sight, this battering . . . I don't know another mother up there who hadn't gotten to the point of saying at one time or another, Everybody go away, leave me alone, let me do it myself. And daddies get pushed away, and I think that's one of the most tragic things about that floor, that daddies get pushed away. Other family members get pushed away.

Because you get to the point where you've just got to hang on, it's all you can do to sustain yourself. There isn't room for anybody else. And I think that's one reason fathers have such a hard time, especially at the end. Because all of a sudden it's the end, guys. You have to come and be a part of this, and they say, "I don't understand . . ."

PSYCHOLOGIST: Who raises the child? The mother.

MOTHER: Well, so does the father.

PSYCHOLOGIST: But in essence it's the mother. Who does the child spend the most time with during the first five years? The mother.

MOTHER: Well, I don't know. In our situation Jerry has always spent a great deal of time with the kids. I was always gone at night. That was my time to go. I stayed during the day. He stayed at night while I went to class. So I have to say in Jerry's case he was very much involved. Not all fathers are that way, I realize.

PSYCHOLOGIST: But most fathers don't take an active part in the caring, the feeding, and the changing of the diapers. I think this is all going to change now, the role of the father/mother, you know, equal duty. The time in the hospital should be spent together so the father feels a part of what is happening. But so many times the fathers get shut out because they choose to be shut out. It's easier. They say, Okay, I'll pay the hospital bill and you stay there with the kid.

MOTHER: A lot choose their job as an escape.

PSYCHOLOGIST: Right. They say, listen we've got to eat. I can't be down here constantly. I've got to work, and that's true, but they ought to be able to share some of the responsibilities and some of the frustrations. In your case, like you say, Jerry came in, and that was good, and that gave you time to spend together and gave Jerry time to spend with Meredith, and yet no matter what you say, Jerry knew he was going to go home on Sunday and go back to the grind and doing normal things, so I think it was easier for him to tolerate the weekend.

And I think it proved the point the weekend you just got up and said, All right, Jerry, you take care of Meredith, the bedpan, the problems, all her gripes. And Jerry realized what you went through during the week. Because he didn't have you there as he usually did on the weekends. He couldn't say, All right, you take care of the bedpan, and I'll go have a cigarette. It's easy to take care of her for an hour while you do the laundry, but how about when she got up fifty times a night and used the bedpan every ten minutes? He became more aware. And he was ready to leave that Sunday. I mean, I said, Jerry, you want to leave at seven? And he said, No, I think I'd better catch the three-o'clock plane! He'd had it. And he said, N., I just can't get the bedpan to the bathroom without going myself, gagging the whole way.

And so the fathers come in when there's not a whole lot of activity. And they never realize what it's like until they have to stay there.

PSYCHOLOGIST: Some children react very emotionally. Some show a great deal of resentment. Some parents make the kid feel it's all their fault.

John's mother exemplified that. Caused severe emotional problems for him [an amputee] at a very impressionable age [thirteen]. And outside of the fact that he was no longer like other boys physically, his mother kept telling him what a bum he was. And he just rebelled against the staff, the people in general. And it took a long time working with him to overcome what his parents had instilled in him—that he was different and that he was going to die, and that he was wasting their time by prolonging it. You wouldn't think you would find that in this type of situation, but you will.

Some of the parents have other problems on top of the child's illness. The illness just complicates things and the parents themselves withdraw. Which causes the child to withdraw.

Other times you find all the parent needs is someone to lean on, who cares what's happening. Someone to talk to. I think that's the greatest deficit on that floor, there's no one to talk to. You have the chaplains who wring their hands and grope for something to say. And the staff, understaffed, too busy to talk, and social service, which can only do so much. And you find a bond among the mothers on the floor, because they're all in the same boat, and yet they all look for someone outside the floor to talk to. Even Bob's mom needed someone to talk to, to help her understand what the doctors were telling her, to help her make decisions, to help accept the fact that Bob was going to die.

A lot of the mothers need a great deal of love. I mean, all mothers love their children. But the love that's shown at that hospital, the love, the affection, the giving the mothers show their children. It's beautiful. The mothers are reaching . . . the children are reaching.

Treatment Decisions

Risks and decisions are part of the daily struggle of caring for a child with a serious disease such as cancer. They may be relatively minor, such as judging whether the child's blood counts are high enough to expose him to crowds or to possible bruises on the playground.

They may be major ones, such as whether or not to withdraw

treatment at some point when hope is minimal and the treatment effects may seem worse than death.

In a parent-care setting, the parent, and at times the child, are often a part of decision-making in one way or another. Obviously, some parents are more able to understand the technical considerations than others, and some parents are more able to make decisions than others. The system isn't perfect. But one of the most comforting resources a parent has is that information and assistance in understanding it are available, even if at times doctors need to be reminded to provide it.

MOTHER: Risks . . . I remember, during Christmas they put Meredith back on prednisone and vincristine, which never did anything for her. I was furious. I was just seething! I thought the kid's got a bad bone marrow, she's not going to get better on something that's never worked before. Not at this point. And I can remember feeling so neglected, so abandoned. I had asked for a conference. I had done everything but kick the doctor's door down. I had told her twice on rounds, I had told you, I told a number of people in authority, everyone I could possibly pin to the wall, I want a conference.

And I realize Dr. S. was getting her thoughts together on what do we do now. Because I'm sure she knew what I was going to say. I wasn't the easiest mother to handle. But I believed very strongly that this was not a valid way to live. And I told her that Jerry and I were of one mind. Let's try something aggressive, and if we have reached the point where there is nothing left to try, then I don't want to put Meredith through it.

Now I realize everybody says that. And you leave the hospital and say, Well, we'll die with dignity, we'll do this together, and at the first fever you come racing back to clinic, full of guilt and everything. And I was glad we didn't have to go through this.

We took an aggressive route. But I spelled out to her what I wanted, and I think had I not, I don't know what would have come, but I don't think it would have been aggressive. I'm not sorry.

COUNSELOR: Oh, no.

MOTHER: Ever.

COUNSELOR: I was at a seminar recently on personhood—and all the women in the group kept wanting to get to the question of, Do you have the right to destroy a fetus? And all the men wanted to get back to the theoretical and philosophical approach. We kept saying this leaves females just where they were left, holding the bag, quite literally.

But this is the question because it happened this week. I was talking to a doctor here, who's not in pediatrics, about a child whose mother has refused treatment. And the child-welfare worker had told me they were going to get a judgment about this child from the court. And this doctor was very incensed that the child-welfare worker had called him for information, and he was telling me we don't want to push this. And I said we're not pushing. This is not our job to push it. But it is our job, if we have conviction about treatment for children, to give information to the people whose job it is to go to court.

And he was saying parents have the right to refuse treatment. And I thought, Well, really, do they? Obviously sometimes the court doesn't think so. Because you know, transfusions and such are sometimes court-ordered, even if it's against the parents' religious beliefs, which is one of the most sacred things in our Constitution, our legal system.

Do you have the right to destroy a fetus, do you have the right to, well, not destroy a child's life, but do you have the right to deliberately withhold treatment when you have been advised that treatment will have some measure of success? I am not talking at all about the terminal kind of situation where most doctors leave it up to parents as well as other families . . .

MOTHER: As to when to stop?

COUNSELOR: Yes, when to stop, although that's a real tricky, queasy kind of question. It's very tricky. And again it depends so much on the individual doctor and his approach, and individual parents. But I'm talking about a deliberate choice. Just not to have any treatment at all. This happened to be x-ray therapy.

MOTHER: I think it could be argued that it might be a terminal situation. That's pretty academic, but I know what you're saying. But there is an argument, legally, the fact that this condition exists is just as terminal as if you'd gone through everything possible and still come up with still a terminal situation. It's just a matter of time.

COUNSELOR: No, I don't think you can say that.

MOTHER: Why, because you think there's always hope?

COUNSELOR: Yes, I do think there's always hope.

MOTHER: Well, I would tend to agree with you as far as my own situation, but I can see someone, well, I know my first reaction when Meredith got sick was, Dear God if she has to die, make it quick! And then of course the longer you're in the situation the longer you hold out and hope and the more you deny . . .

COUNSELOR: Of course.

MOTHER: And the more you say it's really not happening to us. It's really going to be all right. We really are going to make it through this, and survive somehow. And of course, most of us don't.

COUNSELOR: And what you're saying is maybe there's a real argument for no treatment at all.

MOTHER: In the very abstract. But because I have strong ethical feelings about that sort of thing, so it's only in the abstract, but I think it does exist.

COUNSELOR: Well, to me this has always been the thing that makes pediatrics much more difficult. Now, I've always had a very clear-cut feeling about this, say with an amputation, that I think I could perfectly reasonably decide about myself, either treatment/no treatment. Amputation/no amputation. Whatever. Any kind of mutilation.

But to put this upon another person, to decide about their child, you've got another factor here. Because I think people have the right to decide for themselves. I'm not sure whether I have the right, for instance, to decide whether my husband should have treatment. Or my child. Obviously, you can't take a child Meredith's age and let her make the decision. And no child in her right mind would want to be stuck, certainly not to have a leg cut off.

I can understand very well someone saying, I choose, after having all the facts explained . . . If I had osteogenic sarcoma I don't believe I'd have an amputation. But I'd very likely have an amputation on one of my children if they had it. And that probably sounds real crazy.

But I would be so hopeful that maybe this would be one in that 10 percent they tell me make it—I never seem to see them survive—and it's such a miserable way to die, after having been mutilated. I think if I, now knowing what I know, I'd rather die. And yet I wouldn't feel that I could say if there's any chance at all that I could close it off for my child. Does that make any sense to you?

MOTHER: Well, I can understand your feeling, but it's a double standard.

COUNSELOR: Of course it is. Because who has the right to decide about someone else's life?

MOTHER: And you can argue the other way and say I'm not

going to suffer that way but I'll put my child through it. And I think all parents have that same fear.

You know I was glad . . . people were surprised at our reaction to Meredith's death. I had to say in brutal honesty I was glad it happened the way it did. I was glad it was fast. I was glad I didn't have to make major decisions.

The only person who approached me was not a staff member here but my own father, who's a doctor, and he came up to me the last night. We had pretty well figured out it would be that night. And he said, "Do you want any heroics?" And I said, "What do you mean, 'heroics'?" And he said, "Resuscitator. . . ." And I said, "No!" And he was glad, but he wanted us to say it. And after we got the provisional autopsy, I was ever so glad we didn't even try.

But, well, I don't know. I guess parents go through different feelings about stopping treatment. It would have been hard for me. And I always wondered if I went to a doctor at a certain point and said, "What do I do now?" how much help would I get? Are they going to say, Well, in my professional opinion we could do this or do that, and statistically these are the likely results? Well, that's just a bunch of bullshit. It really doesn't tell you anything.

And how do the staff members here help parents make value judgments in areas in which they [parents] have no technical knowledge? How do they do that? How helpful are they? What do you do? I should think that would be one of the toughest areas of this job.

COUNSELOR: It is. Obviously, because the people on the staff are just as ignorant in many ways and just as incapable of knowing about a particular child as the parent is. The best they can do is give an educated guess. So many times, because you know I have sat in on enough conferences, and I know the medical staff would say this, uh, that this one isn't going to make it, and this one *makes* it a little longer. Now that doesn't mean this is really living, in my estimation.

I think it depends of course very much who you talk to. Uh, I've known several doctors who have been quite, quite helpful, and one I know who even encouraged parents to stop treatment. I've known others who would resuscitate, and the rest of the staff would say, Why on earth?

But again this goes back to the value judgments of the individual. Now, there have been situations where this has been decided as a group, we will not do any more. And we will not proceed. That this child really doesn't have anything more in the reserve to draw on.

MOTHER: Is this something they discuss with the parents, or do they just stop doing things that would unnecessarily prolong . . . ?

COUNSELOR: They very often just stop. And I have often suggested to parents that they approach the doctor and talk to them. Uh, this is something that depends on the individual. Some parents will go. Some parents will initiate this.

Talking about Death

COUNSELOR: This is like when you talked with me about funerals, arrangements, and what do you do.

MOTHER: Well, I had to know.

[At the beginning of the relapse period, September 1972.]

COUNSELOR: And so many mothers ask, "What do I do if I'm here alone and this happens?" Then I'm free to talk about it. I just don't feel that it's ever really possible to talk with someone about it until they initiate it. Until they are ready to say it themselves then they are just going to block it out.

MOTHER: I think that's a good way to do it. I had . . . you know,

I'm so open sometimes about my feelings about Meredith and about her death. Especially with some of the mothers on the floor. Particularly Mary and I have talked about many things and gotten a lot of things worked out, and I have found a great deal of help from the other parents.

But what I started to say was, I sent an article to her, I may have sent you one . . . "Walk in the World for Me" [story of a boy with leukemia]. I loved that story. Well, I sent it at some risk, but she thought it was beautiful, too. Several of the people upstairs [pediatrics] read it and passed it around. Evidently one of the nurses, P. or someone in authority, had suggested that Mary share that with some other mother. I don't know who it was. And she said, "Isn't that beautiful?" And the other mother said, "That's the worst thing I ever read in my whole life." She was not ready to discuss this.

COUNSELOR: Sure, sure.

MOTHER: You never know at what point you can approach someone with these things.

Talking about death with doctors was considerably more difficult in most instances than talking with other parents. There have been a number of studies that indicate doctors choose medicine as a career because of an inordinate fear of death. And medicine is dedicated to defeating death.

During the course of Meredith's illness, and my own, we met a number of doctors, each of whom had his or her own way of dealing with the threat of death. One doctor, whom I admire greatly and who, more than any other doctor, probably gave us strength and ability to cope openly with Meredith's leukemia, was the one I felt was least able to deal with the actual death.

A young resident turned out to be one of the most helpful of all. She did not have the gangbusters approach of the previously mentioned doctor. But she very insistently and consistently pointed out the times she felt we should make some definite move.

It was she who convinced me to tell Meredith the name of her disease, what it was and what could be done about it. Later she helped us pick a least-threatening occasion to tell Meredith of the death of one of her little friends. She also was always the one to recognize our needs to let off some emotional steam. And she was always available to talk, even if she didn't have all of the answers.

Another of the "favorite" doctors in Texas was beautifully responsive to our needs, but only when we sought her out and formally presented them.

Still another seemed to delight in giving parents bad news. She had always been very nice to us, and I never really understood why, because I had seen her be nothing short of brutal to others. And I was always sure we would be next. But we never were.

My own doctor, who has such supersensitive antennae that he picks up and responds to every subtle cue around him, becomes resistant at the mention of death. When I was hospitalized and the room was filled with flowers, I jokingly remarked that it looked as if I had already died. His face grew very serious, and he said, "Oh, no! Flowers are a sign of life." He later made several similar remarks.

On another occasion when I referred to MS as a fatal disease, he let me know he did not consider it a proper evaluation. "Potentially fatal?" I asked. "No." "Potentially disabling?" "All right," he said.

Perhaps as patients we expect too much from doctors. We deify them, expect them to be able to recognize and correct every little hurt, allowing very little room for error and virtually none for forgiveness. I can see my own impatience in the comments that follow, comments that in retrospect I see as a little harsh, but they were honest feelings I had six weeks after Meredith's death. I hasten to add I hold all the doctors mentioned in very high regard, although my critical focus at the time was only concerned with how they handled death. Now I am willing to accept any human failing in a doctor except refusal to talk at all, or outright deceit.

COUNSELOR: Dr. S. particulary gets lots of clues from parents. I don't think that means she doesn't know what she thinks is best medically, but I think it's her own personality. That if she knows parents really have convictions about something. For instance, she is very amenable to letting people go home. If they really want to go home. Much more so than, say, Dr. W. was. In a very different kind of way.

MOTHER: I really love Dr. W., but I think he was so terrified of death. He just screamed this to me—"I'm afraid!"

COUNSELOR: That's right, that's right. And he just couldn't give up! Way past the point where it made any sense to the rest of us. And at the point where people were really telling him, just let them go. So many times it's obvious, or it seems to be obvious to me that people are really ready. They're ready for the child to die. The child is ready. And I think to actively prolong beyond this point is just unnecessary torture for everybody.

This was the thing that I always found so personally difficult. Because there were so many things about his philosophy of care that I liked.

MOTHER: Oh, I do, too.

COUNSELOR: I know you do. But it was this factor, this inability to consider the fact that this child is going to die, which I felt so many times blocked off the closeness that can come when you really consider that you might lose, because you know you might. And when you say you won't and can't, then as you say, you're just denying. There's nothing positive about that.

MOTHER: I agree. You know, I've seen his hospital. And it's a beautiful hospital. And at the time I thought, Well, I wish I hadn't seen it. I have it on my mind, to make a decision. When we got home from there and a few days later Meredith relapsed, I thought, I have to make this decision now. And we chose to come back here [Houston]. And part of it, I think, was resisting the personality influence of Dr. W., whom I like. And I loved the hospital. It's beautiful, but I thought, When it really comes right down to it, what's going to happen to Meredith? And I felt she was better off here. For me, I'd be better off there! And when I thought of it in those terms it made all the difference in the world. And that's not to put him down at all, because I think he really has a fine thing going. And it will be finer yet. He may overrun you guys soon. But at the time that's what I felt.

You know, when we first came to Houston he was at a meeting, and there was a family that kept saying, "Oh, wait till you meet Dr. W., he has such a great positive mental attitude." And on and on. "And he just lifts your spirits." Well, he did. After talking with him I just felt great. But five minutes later you had to pick me up off the floor. And I thought, that's bullshit, that's 90 percent bullshit.

COUNSELOR: Uhm, hmm. That's right.

MOTHER: And I have heard him say so many times, in a very critical situation—because he always discussed things at the foot of the bed . . .

COUNSELOR: Yes, sure.

MOTHER: I mean, it was this great conflict of personality traits. He's afraid to acknowledge that this child is going to die, but he'll stand at the foot of the bed and discuss every gory detail.

COUNSELOR: Everything! As if the whole picture . . .

MOTHER: As if it's going to be all right. And I've heard him say many times, Well, if this doesn't work, we'll try something else. That's the stock answer.

COUNSELOR: Certainly.

MOTHER: And the one time I know of in a death situation, where it was the day the parents withdrew drugs, and there was no, absolutely no hope, and he just walked in the room and said, "Well, I'm leaving for a meeting. You may be here when I get back and you may not." And walked out. And I thought what kind of a, well, I'm sorry, I just thought that was kind of a letdown. I mean, I felt that this was not very supportive. In light of previous promises. Does that make sense?

COUNSELOR: Yeah.

MOTHER: And when I went in with Dr. S. for that last conference, I said, This is what we want. Well, I said, where are we? And she said, Well things are not too good, but they are not altogether without hope. So she gave me a choice. Whereas Dr. W. always said, Well, we'll try something else. Dr. S. . . . I've criticized her for her aloofness, but we really talk well. I can really communicate with the woman. It's just getting in there that's difficult. I really don't know how she does all she does.

COUNSELOR: It's not only getting in there. It's getting her. Because I think that, I mean getting her to really listen to you. If you can . . . she usually will respond. But she has, I think for so many reasons, built up something that's almost impenetrable at times. And unless a person keeps after it, many times a parent will just get completely defeated. If she doesn't come around and volunteer information, they just quit. I personally can't conceive of that. You consider yourself, I would be beating down the door. I want to know. And she really was wanting to have that conference with you, but she does this, sometimes hesitates, which I think is wise, and perhaps she's always been this way. Of course, I didn't know her except during the time Dr. W. was here, but I think because he tended to be so much the other way it activated in her this resistance to give false kinds of reassurance. And so not wanting to tell you the bad news, she sometimes doesn't tell you anything. And leaves you just hanging there wondering, my God, what is happening?

MOTHER: There's a great deal of discord on the floor about that sort of thing.

COUNSELOR: Of course.

MOTHER: Not so much with the new parents. They don't know any better. As the old parents leave and the new parents come on, there's not so much complaining. But, boy, you should have heard the gripes last fall when a bunch of us came in who had been in before! And we were angry!

COUNSELOR: Sure.

MOTHER: Really angry!

COUNSELOR: And of course I can be sympathetic with doctors. They are trained to defeat death. And unfortunately some of them like Dr. W. don't learn. And I get that feeling myself sometimes, which sounds pretty idiotic. I see some kid come into clinic, and I get so angry! Just so angry at, like the disease, itself. Like, you take this as a defeat, when a child dies, and you can't help but feel the loss.

The last day of Meredith's life, the doctors became even more attentive.

MOTHER: I think when Meredith went comatose that morning, I wasn't fully aware that that's what it was. I mean, I knew it but I didn't, and when doctors made rounds that morning they were so obvious about it . . . they went clear to the end of the hall, skipped us, zigzagged back, and that's not their normal route. A bunch of them.

And Mrs. B. cried, and said, "I'm so sorry." And she put

her arm around me. I can't believe how cool I was at the time, but I just said, "I don't want her to hurt anymore."

And the head nurse cried, and she left. And Dr. S. explained the technical things that were happening. And nothing more was said until that night. And Dr. M. came in and asked how long she had been in a coma. I said, "Since this morning." And she was not her usual prophet of doom. She just turned and left. And she told B. [a nurse] . . . didn't you overhear this? She said, "This is it. Tonight's the night." My father said the same thing.

PSYCHOLOGIST: Yes. I went back out into the hall, and B. and Y. [nurses] were out there, but Dr. M. pulled me by the collar of my jacket and was not at all very diplomatic with me, and she asked me where I was going, and told me not to go, that Meredith was going to die that night. And immediately B. and Y. came up and said Dr. M. had been known to be wrong before.

And it was at that point, Dr. M. made a point for me to tell you, and I asked you to come out on the back staircase [the only private place for a conversation].

MOTHER: She told you to tell me? Why didn't *she* tell me? She certainly never hesitated to tell anybody else.

PSYCHOLOGIST: I don't know.

MOTHER: She's said some pretty rough things to parents. But she never did to me.

PSYCHOLOGIST: Well, she asked me to tell you.

MOTHER: I can think back . . . did you ever know Susan, a teenager . . . she was our roomie once—had tumors. And she was really a neat kid, but she'd had vincristine problems so bad, she couldn't walk without leaning against the wall. And the next time she came back in she had tumors everywhere. And Dr. X. took her aside and told her—she was fourteen or fifteen—and told her she was going to die. And I thought that was really, you know, a great thing to do.

Now you can't tell a six-year-old, but you can tell their parents. And I think I was angry that this was not being done right now. I knew what was happening, and yet there was a certain level where I wouldn't admit it.

I can remember the day after Meredith went on critical, and I had gone to pick up my dad at the air terminal, and come back, and I was walking down the hall for coffee and Dr. R. called to me from the treatment room, and said, "Mrs. Elliott, did anyone ever explain what this means, going on critical?" And I said, "Well, I have a pretty good idea! But nobody ever sat down and told me." And he was upset about that. He said, "Well, someone should have told you just exactly what this means. She's very near death." He was very kind about it, but also very explicit. And he told me all the things that were wrong physiologically, and we sat around and discussed what if she would die, what if she would survive . . . because I really was worried that if she survived she would have brain damage.

But I thought, Why didn't somebody tell me? It wouldn't hurt to tell me, really.

Children's Awareness of Death

One of the most difficult aspects of Meredith's illness was not that she was aware of the seriousness of her leukemia, but that she did not always share her worries with us. I was hurt. I felt as if we had failed in helping her cope with her worries about death. Somehow, though, that "important friend" always entered the scene, as if on cue, to catch a barrage of serious questions. If a friend weren't handy, it might be a babysitter or an unsuspecting salesclerk. But mothers were universally protected.

PSYCHOLOGIST: One day [during Meredith's initial hospitalization] I got the question, What lives and what dies? So we talked about that, and a week later she asked me what I was doing in the afternoon . . . she didn't want to stay by herself while you went to pick up Jerry at the airport. So I said I'd stop down. She started throwing questions at me, everything she'd bottled up for the entire week.

So she wanted to know if just old people died. And we talked about the life cycle, and I used the rose as an example. How a rose starts out as a bud, develops into a flower, and it's very beautiful. And it gives a lot to the world and to people who love flowers. Eventually the rose loses its petals and leaves and it dies.

Then again, Do people go through life and then die when they get old? So we had to backtrack. . . . I said sometimes insects come and destroy the flower before it gets a chance to go through the cycle. And in essence this is what happens when a child is ill.

She said, "Well, then children die." And I said, "Well, you get a flower with insects on it, what do you do . . . you spray it. And sometimes you don't catch it soon enough and the flower dies. But if you catch it soon enough the flower will be healthy again and go through its normal cycle."

She had a couple more questions, but she worked it through, that some things die, some don't, that you don't have to be old to die.

In treating the child if they can't comprehend life and death, they can comprehend an analogy, like the rose. And I was someone who wore a white uniform and knew about leukemia. At the same time I never gave her a shot or caused her any physical pain like nurses, doctors, and I was not a threat . . .

MOTHER: Well, this is about dying in general . . . she and I first discussed it, well we discussed it when two of her friends died a year earlier, and then not again for a while because she was in good health and it wasn't (apparently) a threat . . . then in April when I got sick and . . . I had the same tests she did, and she got a big kick out of that. And then when the tests were back, and I told her I have this disease, MS, and that I will always have it. I was trying to point out the similarities of the two diseases, and yet they weren't similar, but I was saying I'll have this the rest of my life, and someday it may kill me.

And this is when we got into the discussion of time. And I think I finally got across to her, that it was so many years anyway. And I said, Well, think what would it be like if my mother died today when I'm all grown up. I'd be sad, but I don't need my mother to take care of me, so it's not the same as if she died when I was little and needed her to take care of me. She understood that. And she had the strangest reaction. She thought it was just great that we were sick together. And we'd be in remisison together and relapse together. And I think she understood the time concept in that sense, that it's not going to affect her as far as being dependent.

PSYCHOLOGIST: She only mentioned how she felt about your MS once. Something klutsy you did. I made a remark, and she chewed me out for it. She didn't seem to have any big hang-ups about it, and that she might need you and you wouldn't be there.

MOTHER: That's one thing I always promised her, that I would be there. I often wondered if that frightened her, that I could only promise her that one thing. I never promised anything else. Maybe kids need more security than that.

PSYCHOLOGIST: She never talked to you about separation?

MOTHER: I think sometimes she thought I was going to be so dependent on . . . it doesn't take that much to make you dependent on . . . it doesn't. That's the worst thing about parent care, the dependency. The kids get used to having Mommy right there. And she used to get mad when I would leave the room. And I wondered if she felt I was abandoning her when I went to parents' meetings, or across the street to get something to eat.

PSYCHOLOGIST: I have my own philosophy about that . . . but the mothers tend to bend over backwards; if they go out for a cigarette or to fix dinner they take too long—in the forty-second microwave oven. And this is the child's way of letting off some steam.

I don't think Meredith ever felt abandoned, at any time during her entire illness. I think parents' meeting was a way of giving kids a chance to gripe. It wasn't exclusive with Meredith. Something very common on that floor with all the mothers.

You know, grown-ups like to have it put down in black and white. Meredith and kids like her say so much more, by watching and listening. Take from them all they're willing to give, and they do give so much, in a way adults are unable to perceive. . . . Many people just let it slip by, and, in essence what she was telling you for two years was how she felt about having cancer or leukemia.

She really did express her fears and anxieties and hopes. And she did show us she was courageous and that she wasn't always sure this was the way she wanted it. That she was just a little kid and didn't have any rights as a citizen. She had nothing to say about whether or not she took her treatment. Really. Legally.

Every one of those kids knows what's happening to them inside, because you can feel it. It's just like you knew you had MS before your diagnosis. At Christmas I knew there was something wrong with my leg and there was no way medically that . . . it's something you know that's inside of you, and these kids experience it more than adults because they don't repress the same things an adult represses.

Some researchers have said that when the body is close to death, a signal goes out to let the person know. Meredith knew, but again she protected me. During the previous five months since her relapse she had asked me to tell her about funerals until we had thoroughly exhausted the subject. Suddenly there were no more questions directed to me. But from her friend she demanded the answers . . . Do people die alone? Do they wear clothes? What are funerals about? If I die, will you come to my funeral? And she clearly spelled out her wishes—what she was to wear and keep with her, and where she was to be buried ("aboveground").

MOTHER: How did Meredith reveal to you that she knew she was going to die?

PSYCHOLOGIST: First there was a series of attitude changes. The most drastic was when she came back to Houston after Christmas. She was aware of what leukemia was all about, the fatality rate, and yet she assured herself that she would beat it. After Christmas it was more of a defeatist attitude, that she would never leave the hospital.

MOTHER: The changes during Christmas. The bone marrow was out of sequence . . . she cried for the very first time. People at home said later that it was the first time they were really aware she was so sick. And she was terrified. She said things like, "Can you die if you don't have any polys?" And we had to go through the difference between not having enough polys and not having enough blood, like if you cut your wrists or something and bleed to death. She'd had no polys before, and it hadn't concerned her that much. This time she said she was going to die.

PSYCHOLOGIST: There was a letdown. I don't know what happened, whether it was Wichita, or returning to Houston. She spent most of her time in Houston as an out-patient. And being in the hospital always made a change in her attitude.

MOTHER: Somehow you always hate to go in [the hospital], but once you're in, you hate to leave. It's very secure.

The only thing she said to me, beside this poly business, was that she was afraid . . . just afraid.

PSYCHOLOGIST: That last week she did admit to me she was afraid she was going to die. At the hospital. She had sent you out of the room and she was going to tell me all the things you had done wrong that day and why she was so disgusted with you. Nothing was right. She was afraid.

Meredith wanted me to tell you all you had done wrong, to punish you for going to parents' meeting. And after she went through all the little things she said, she was afraid she might die.

MOTHER: Earlier . . . during our wait for conference, we were both depressed. She asked me, "Can you die of a bad bone marrow?" And I said, "Yes, but it takes a long time."

I can't pin down any experience, any event that happened to make her change her attitude at the last except that last bone marrow. She had decided that had to be a good bone marrow. Maybe she was just tired. You can only fight so long and then things get pretty discouraging. And just everything that happened toward the last there, like the smock [N.'s Christmas gift], about how she knew she was never going to make it out of the hospital to wear the smock. . . . I wonder how she knew that.

I think she kind of gave up. Hanging on really wasn't worth it. Life could not be normal. It was unbelievably important to her that she not be so different. The security, like Mary says, life in the hospital is rough, but in her case she has a houseful of healthy children at home. And although they want Jim at home, he's happy in the hospital. He can't keep up with the others.

PSYCHOLOGIST: I don't think Meredith ever felt she couldn't keep up.

MOTHER: Yes, I think she did.

The Team

Early in Meredith's remission, our young psychologist friend paid us a visit. Later she admitted that one of the reasons for her trip was to finish some research. Another was to say good-bye.

MOTHER: I'll never forget that visit. You got sick. Cracked up your car. I had to tell Meredith you weren't feeling well, and I promised you I wouldn't tell her why. The drive back to Dallas. I was grieving.

PSYCHOLOGIST: I think you reacted normally considering the circumstances. Mothers are very protective.

MOTHER: Well, it started out that way. I had my little speech all written. I had forgotten that. I think the most important thing that came out of that was my feeling toward you, and cancer, and maybe I was projecting, but I'd forgotten what my original speech was all about until now. I was telling you to stay away from my kid. I said, Why did you come? And you said, Because this is the last time. And my reaction was, Stay away from my kid. Don't die. Don't you hurt my child.

And I think I realized for the first time . . . well, I was mad that you came, really was, aggravated about the whole thing . . . and uh, 'cause I didn't really know you very well, and you just announced one day that you were coming, and I thought, gee.

Then we ended up driving back to Dallas together with a

broken car. That was the most intense six hours I ever spent in my life. And to know that you were going to die, and that I really did feel something for you, that you were not just a young kid who came in and gave Meredith suckers all the time against my better judgment. And I, wow, when I got on the plane that night, I wept all the way back to Witchita. It was a long flight. I cried half the next day. And for the next week I wasn't worth a damn. I truly grieved then. It was my first grief experience [since Meredith's diagnosis]. It was sudden, intense, and very thorough. And I don't know if I was grieving in part for you and in part for her. I just know it was a grief experience. It was very intense. I can remember from that point on our fighting a lot.

PSYCHOLOGIST: We always fought a lot.

MOTHER: We fought more between the time in October when you came up and said you were sick and *might* die, and January in Houston when you said you were sick and probably *will* die. And that day in the airport . . .

You know, the thing about Meredith's dying that made it more acceptable was that we had time to prepare as much as one can prepare. And I was ready as much as I could be ready. And I think the first two times you told me you were going to die, I wasn't ready. And I was saying, You can't do that, it's not fair. I haven't had time.

And my first reaction . . . remember that day you came into the clinic between Christmas and New Year's and your tumor had ruptured, and you said, Man, this could really be it, maybe a month. And my reaction was, you cannot do that to my child. You can't die. You've toyed with her emotions, you've stolen her heart. And you won't let me tell her about you. I just thought, Screw you. And I said, Either you tell her or I will. It wasn't fair to her.

And I don't understand why you were so terrified of this.

All the way along you kept making me promise not to say anything to her, and I still don't understand what's such a big deal about it. She saw other people die of cancer.

[mumbled response]

But, you know, I think that was one of the strongest things in the whole team. Eventually it was because we all leveled with each other about our health. And after you told her about your tumors that day in the airport—that was the hardest—I never had such a hard time getting on an airplane. Remember how she reached up and hugged you spontaneously? And I thought, God, well, she's saying good-bye, and that's really what I had in mind. And I think that's the worst thing I ever went through in my life. I was really choked up.

It was all I could do to get her on the plane. And as we were sitting there . . . and I really thought she'd had it figured out by this time, I thought she was aware from all our talk about chemotherapy and being zapped, and all the little hints we dropped. She never put it together and I thought she had. And she said, "I didn't know N. had a tumor." I say, "Yes." Long silence. And she said, "People don't die of tumors, do they?" I said, "Well, sometimes they do and sometimes they don't." She said, "I hope N. doesn't die." And I said, "I hope so, too." And then she didn't say too much about it until we got home. Jerry picked us up and that was the great announcement of the evening . . . N. has a tumor.

We didn't discuss it in any depth until you got the next one. When I went to Austin [May 1972] to see you, I told her where I was going, that you were very sick. I didn't say you might die, I just said you were really very sick, and that she couldn't go this trip, but go to Grandma's this weekend. I know she was very much aware that you might die then, and that you almost did shortly thereafter, and she knew that, and

I think the fact that you didn't die, that you made it, was a great source of strength to her. And it was a risk, yes, but it paid off. She saw that you almost died several times, but that you made it.

This is another reason that it kind of disturbs me that she gave up. She really did give up.

Normalcy

If there is one groping emotional need among these stricken children, it is to be like other children. Some admittedly would rather be dead than different. Striving for normalcy requires a valiant effort. Achieving it is its own greatest reward. Yet, most families I have met did achieve it to an amazing degree. From a personal standpoint, I feel that achieving normalcy was the force that carried our family through the crisis with dignity. And we had the satisfaction that we all lived the time together with double our share of enjoyment because we knew we might never have a "normal" experience together again.

MOTHER: There was a point during Christmas, which was a very bad time for us, where we all began to sense that this was really the end, and I do think in the long run Meredith gave up, and she was tired, and didn't want to live this way any longer. We had passed that point where you cannot achieve normalcy, and she said forget it.

COUNSELOR: That's when I think people *should* say forget it.

MOTHER: She did, she really did. And I realize it more now than I did at the time. But I can really see it working now.

COUNSELOR: So in a very real sense the child does choose.

MOTHER: She did choose. I feel very strongly about it.

COUNSELOR: You know the thing I think that was so beautiful in that story ["Walk in the World for Me"], and I think this applies to any mother with adolescents, children, as I have, and you will be having soon, is the ability this woman had to let that kid do all kinds of god-awful things. I think that was the thing that really kept coming through to me. That what a strong, great kind of person she had to be, to let him do those things. And how he was able to. Because you know any adolescent boy has just gotta take risks. If you don't allow them to take risks, you know, driving or whatever, then you are just wrecking them.

MOTHER: You have to take the risks with the little ones, too. We did it, too. There were times we went to movies, or in crowds to do some dumb thing that I couldn't have cared less about because I felt it was important to Meredith. I think this was the biggest factor, and I think we had an intensely beautiful relationship, for all the crap we had to go through for nineteen months. It was a beautiful experience in many ways. I have to say that was a part of it. But it was a part at great risk. We took a lot of risks.

Meredith's friend felt strongly about being normal, too.

PSYCHOLOGIST: Maybe that's what turned Meredith to me and I to her, but she did respect normalcy, and so do I. When you have cancer, your first impulse is, I've got to cram a whole lot of living into a small amount of time. And all of a sudden you stop dead in your tracks and say, But I'll never beat it. And, oh well, you go to Europe and play around, you know, just screw around a lot, cram a lot of living into a short prognosis.

But it's not too long before you find out that's not the way to do it. I said, If I'm in A-1 perfect health, what would I do? I'd go back to school and get my degree and carry on from there. And I did. And I think that meant a lot to Meredith, too, to go to school, to be like other kids, and I can empathize with how she felt. She wasn't going to be able to beat it and go back and be with the kids and live a normal life. And this is what she wanted to do. School became an obsession, as if she were saying, I can be normal if I can go back to school. I want to be like everybody else. I'm tired of being laughed at, tired of IVs and tired of people asking me why I have needles.

I can empathize with that.

A lot of diseases are cruel and hard, but I don't think any of them equal the dehumanization process that a cancer or leukemia patient goes through. You're not only slowly being eaten away inside, but at the same time your personality changes and you are dehumanized.

Many patients are lucky. They have no obvious deformity. I went through a rough period last May where all of a sudden I was faced with what kind of person am I going to be with only one leg. And it was probably the hardest part of my entire . . . There were times when I wanted to give up and say to hell with it, it's not worth it. And there were times I would say, Well, if I have any kind of inner strength, any kind of character, if I value the true meaning of life, then life without one leg is not going to matter.

I think you can draw a comparison with some of the kids on the floor that have been through this. The kids with severe deformities, the maxillofacials. You see a tremendous amount of change. And exactly where do you draw the line for quality of life? It really is individual. It's what you want to gain out of life.

What happened to Meredith about normalcy? The very first I think was that you started putting down restrictions. She couldn't go into open places because of blood counts. Well, normal people go anywhere, and it made her very aware of her illness. And say, Well, you can't go to school today because there are three kids with the measles.

Meredith's first really big setback was when she lost her hair, and the other kids laughed at her.

MOTHER: Losing the hair. No big deal, except the first time is murder. Of course, she didn't lose it when we expected her to. She lost it ten months later. It just all came out one day. Whammo. And we both sat down and cried.

The hair business was a trauma from all kinds of standpoints. She always wore a wig to school after that, but she never wore one anywhere else. The grocery store, or anywhere. She'd rip it off, say it was hot and scratchy and she never put it back on until she went to school. But it was very important to her that she wear it to school and look like other children. And most of the other children knew. Of course all the kids in her class knew she had no hair, and they never teased her about it. At the very last when she got so heavy on prednisone, they asked her about why she was so fat, but the hair business they seemed to be very protective about.

One day three little black girls who were bused into that school, and really angry about it, they cornered her and teased her about her wig, and threatened to take it off, and I think that was about the most terrifying thing that happened to her during school, to be held up to public ridicule because she was different. It was rough getting out of that one. One of her little friends came and got her and took her back to the room. She was really shaken up about it. The funny thing is that the next time she lost her hair, you remember it had grown out a little and looked so cute, well, it didn't really bother her.

PSYCHOLOGIST: You know when we first started going to El Patio [Mexican restaurant], she thought that was a big deal, but after that guy made such an ass out of himself [the head waiter escorted her to the boy's restroom] she really never wanted to go back.

MOTHER: I never realized. . . .

PSYCHOLOGIST: And the very thought of going to El Patio just put her in a rage. Every time we mentioned El Patio she'd get very defensive. Because she got sent to the men's room, and the guy made such a big deal about her arm, and she finally told him she had leukemia. Kids realize what's happening. He made a big fuss over her, treated her differently because she had leukemia.

MOTHER: She always had the greatest put-down. She really knew how to shut people up quickly. They'd say, "Oh, what's wrong with you?" And she'd say, "I have leukemia." And it would stun them so badly, that well, we never had any more trouble.

PSYCHOLOGIST: The things that happened to her did make a difference. When she came to Austin, she said there was a little boy who had a patch on his eye, and that she understood how he felt. People made fun of him because he was different. . . . Meredith and I talked about, well, it doesn't make any difference what people think because people that really matter are not going to care if you have hair or not. And this is when we went through the thing with the Kappas.

[In the spring of 1972 Meredith went through a difficult six-week period of physical illness and depression in the aftermath of a heavy drug reinforcement of her remission. In an effort to lift her spirits we made a trip to Austin, Texas, to see her faithful friend, and the University of Texas sorority, which had showered her with affection and constant attention for the entire school year. She even was invited to their scholarship banquet, where she was presented with an "award" for the best kindergarten grades in the chapter. The visit did not erase the devastating effects of the drugs. Only time healed that. But she did learn that people outside her family would love her even if she looked different.]

PSYCHOLOGIST: The Kappas [she thought] were no longer going

to love her because she didn't have any hair. And it really did make a big difference to her, because Meredith, at that point, realized how much I loved her. And yet when she lost her hair she was afraid to tell me. Meredith was always so proud of her long hair, too. . . .

MOTHER: We had something to joke about. When her hair started to grow back and it was so cute, and you couldn't keep your hands off it. Everybody rubbed their hands over her head. We used to call it "being stroked." And she loved to be stroked.

PSYCHOLOGIST: Yeah, sometimes when she was mad she'd say, "You haven't stroked me all day." And it was so soft, and she was proud of it. It was a blessing, and she started to regain her confidence, but then she got knocked right back off her feet again. She got her hair back and then she started to gain so much weight. . . .

MOTHER: And that was much worse than the hair, really.

PSYCHOLOGIST: And there it went. And she went through this terrible period of hating herself. I have to admit, I was not that taken back when I saw her for the first time without hair.

MOTHER: Well, you were used to seeing kids without hair.

PSYCHOLOGIST: And my father doesn't have a whole lot, either.

But I was taken back when I saw Meredith excessively heavy in the fall. My first impression was, How is that little heart going to pump, keep that body going? She was really hyper about it. One day when I picked her up and said, "Gee, Mere, you must be losing weight, you're not nearly as hard to put on the bed." And she was just fine all morning.

And Meredith did not like not having any control over these things. Like her weight. And her hair. She liked to be her own person. And she couldn't be.

And then we ran into a discipline problem. That stemmed from a lot of things, but one of them was she wanted to prove her normalcy and she needed this extra, constant reassurance.

MOTHER: You know, it was funny, but Meredith never seemed to me to need the same kind of reassurance and confidence-building that so many kids need. Not abnormal kids, I mean things that all kids need while they're learning. Reassurance that what they're doing is right. That they're trying, and they can make mistakes, and they aren't bad if they make mistakes. Meredith didn't usually need that. She had unusual self-confidence, except, until that last fall. Then she needed constant help, in understanding that she had any worth at all.

PSYCHOLOGIST: Yes. She went through a period where she couldn't do anything wrong without really getting mad at herself. I had to sit down and explain to her that everybody makes mistakes. She thought it was abnormal. If she made a mistake she'd say, "Well, how was I supposed to know that?" And she wasn't supposed to know, and she really got mad. She expected herself to know everything. She was harder on herself than anyone else could have been.

Discipline

PSYCHOLOGIST: One of the most difficult areas of parent-child care is discipline. When do you discipline and when don't you?

MOTHER: It's very hard to maintain normal discipline when you think the child is not going to live to reap the benefits. You know, why deprive them? Give them all you can while they're still alive. It's very, very hard to do. And of course the dependency doesn't help, either.

PSYCHOLOGIST: I think the kids reach out, they test you. They know if they were home they would not be allowed to do such and such, to write on the walls. I think many times Meredith was crying out to be disciplined. And even when she thought we were terribly hard on her, and she let the whole world know, she knew she was treated like anyone else. I think if Mere hadn't been disciplined in the fall, you would have run into a lot of what Jan is going to run into with Madge. Meredith knew how much she could get away with. Madge knows she can get away with everything. Discipline is very important toward the end. And I think Meredith made it easy on everybody. She disciplined herself.

She became less and less dependent. She had made her decision, and she was to carry it out in the manner she thought best. That's like saying she knew what the hell was going to happen, and maybe she didn't know exactly *what* would happen, but she handled it in her own way because she still had her own identity. You didn't give in all the time. You disciplined her to let her keep her identity. That's the point of discipline. That helped her make her decisions. She didn't have to depend on you to do every little thing.

Sometimes I don't know if I can do that. Last spring, I got so disgusted with cancer. I said no more cytoxan, no more anything, and I got [from Meredith], "Well how do you expect me to fight if you won't?"

MOTHER: How did she know you quit?

PSYCHOLOGIST: She heard me talking with a friend.

The Last Days

MOTHER: Can we go over again the things that happened the weekend that she died? This whole period, the month before she died, after we came back to Houston, was so different. We came back with the expectation, with the realization, that things were different and not really knowing why. And then she got pneumonia. I'll never forget when she came in that day after we'd gone out to the apartment. It was just a wreck, and I was so angry we couldn't stay there. And I was taking all my anger out on these absent strangers who came into the apartment and took all our things and left the place a mess. We didn't have anything left and we had to go to a motel. And be in public places. And by Sunday morning she was running a fever.

And she came padding into the bathroom that morning, and said, "I don't really want to tell you this"—and I could tell she was just terrified—"but I know I have to. My shoulder hurts." And I think you could have thrown a bucket of whitewash on me. It would have had the same effect. And I tried very hard not to let her know I was really concerned. I said, "Well, we have to go back into the hospital today anyway, and we'll get it taken care of then." But she really hurt, and all I could think of was, That's what happened to Jim. His first symptom was that his shoulder hurt. And I thought, man, I knew it right then, that the drug was going to wipe out the bone marrow at the same time the pneumonia really took hold. It was like a premonition, the week just flashed before me. And that's pretty much what happened.

It seems to be the standing joke on the floor now. You know, we were in that room down at the end of the hall, the "well" end of the hall, with Madge and Barb. And Madge went as an out-patient, and Barb went home, and Y. [a nurse] came down and said, "How would you like to move to a private room?" Which immediately threw me into a panic. [One moved from one end of the hall to the other according to the seriousness of the condition.] And I said, "For medical or for social reasons?" And she assured me it was for social reasons, a "difficult" child was coming in, and that I had a choice of staying or moving. And either it was a very strange coincidence, or she really put one over on me. I can't help think of it really as a coincidence, but it's sort of been the talk of "the family" that's left there, the standing joke is, "Is this for medical or social reasons?" And I think moving to the "sick" end of the hall had an effect on her.

I can't remember what day we moved down there. Must have been Thursday. Running a high fever in the morning. Good in the afternoon. We had a day or two in that room before she got bad. And then we called Jerry to come give white cells. And I can remember when I picked him up. He hadn't planned on coming that weekend. I said, "Well, she's really sick, but she's not *that* sick." Like I really knew it, but was denying it. . . . And by the next morning she was on critical.

And the oxygen. I kept wondering why they didn't bring it before. She felt so bad. She hurt so bad. All over.

PSYCHOLOGIST: She was very aware of what was happening that week.

MOTHER: I can remember when she started to slip away, when she went on critical. And she began saying strange things, like she was dreaming. And I called my dad, and we hassled about whether he should come. And a friend called from San Antonio, and I said, "Well, we've pulled through worse than this before." And she said she told her M.D. husband, and he said, "It's all over." He was so far away, he knew just from what I'd said that it was very likely that things were going to happen all at the same time. And when my dad got there he said, "Gee, she's really not as bad as I thought she would be." But she was by that night [Sunday]. That night he even called Jerry back from the motel. But she just hung in there. She hung in there for a day after we thought she would die. And that business about the leukapheresis that night. It makes me so angry sometimes that the hospital shuts down on the weekends. And she could have had white cells Saturday, if they really wanted her to. We had to wait until Monday, and it was too late then.

And I can remember the way she made that funny noise when she breathed, and every time she made it, I hurt. And Dr. R. kept saying it was just a reflex. Worry about it when she stops doing it. And she stopped doing it Monday.

That night, I fell asleep and woke up just before it was over. And how I thought when she really did die—I knew it was coming—but I couldn't believe it. I asked my dad, "Is she dead?" And he said, "Yes, clinically." And I cried.

Now here I'd said, Please let's get it over with. And when she did die I was just as broken up and just as confused as anyone. Taken totally by surprise. It shocked me that I would have that reaction when I knew perfectly well what was going on.

And they made me leave the room, and I was angry. I thought, gee, they let Ginny stay and clean up Tom, and I really thought they'd let me do that. . . . She's my kid and I have the right to be with her. But they didn't see it that way.

It all happened so fast. I remember going in and talking to Mary after it was over. And she keeps saying that everyone was amazed at how well I accepted it, but I really was in shock. I just went in and told her that it was all over. We talked for a few moments.

I remember nurses came in. I went out earlier to say goodbye to them at the nurses' station. Sometimes I think the staff has a harder time dealing with this than the parents do. And yet they don't have such a hard time with everyone. And I don't understand what it was with Meredith because she wasn't there that long. She couldn't possibly have impressed that many people. But she did. I just can't believe that people who work there get that broken up about everyone who dies.

Not that everyone went to pieces, but there were significant people who cried openly.

Expectations

I have to admit, there was a certain comfort in knowing how it all would end. There was time to prepare. Time to live life to the fullest with as much normalcy as possible. Options were narrowed. Then it was a matter of pursuing the choices. That elusive quality of life that's so fashionable a topic of discussion today.

We were fortunate to have a daughter who had unusual maturity and ability to accept what she knew to be her fate. Yet, it may be one more side effect of cancer that its child-victims grow up very, very fast, for I have seen it happen in many others.

And at the end, it was easier for us than for many others. Not that it was really easy—just easy by comparison. We, my husband and I, knew where we stood at that stage of the disease. We asked for and received the type of aggressive treatment we wanted, assuming full responsibility for the risk. We lost. It was painful and agonizing, but it was swift, and with consent, and with no regrets.

I have seen other children die from cancer. Some lingered, got weaker, and just withered away. Others died from massive, putrid, obscene infections. Those of us whose children died between those extremes must be considered fortunate. Death was not so swift as to rob us of any preparation, nor so prolonged as to devastate us for the rest of our lives.

And with few exceptions every parent I met in the pediatric cancer subculture greeted death with blessed relief. Not one could ever conceive of feeling relief *before* the child died. But when death finally occurred, there was an almost universal feeling of unshackling, of freedom to live without fear and pain again, both for themselves and for their dead children.

MOTHER: Ours happened so fast. So much faster than I expected. I had my mind fixed on Easter. We'll make it till spring, I thought. And, man, it was all over in January. But it was amazing. I can see the change in my own emotions over the weekend. She got pretty sick on Friday, really sick on Saturday. Panic, anxiety, and acceptance, in three days.

COUNSELOR: Yeah!

MOTHER: I remember the day you came in. I'm ready. I'm not ready, but I'm as ready as I'm going to be. And please let's get it over with. And I got very antsy and anxious and I thought, How long is this going to last?

Quality of Life

MOTHER: Let me ask you . . . some questions about in-service training for staff.

COUNSELOR: You get what you can. Actually I think the best kind of training is, uh, experience. But there is a special emphasis put on that [dying] here, especially in the nursing department. It's very good. They're continually trying to learn new techniques, new ways of dealing with people who are dying. And I think from my standpoint that so much is this a problem in our whole society. We all are conditioned not to think about death. And my own feeling is that only when they can face death can they really live. Because death is so much a part of living. But so much of our population spends a considerable amount of energy trying to deny death.

But we're all going to die. We know that really. And so many times how or why isn't important if we can just catch on to the point that it's how we live.

It's like when I first had to go to work when my children

were so small and I had all kinds of struggle with this, and guilt, and I finally had to realize that there were some days I stayed home all day that I wasn't with my children at all. I was burdened and harassed and worried about money, mad and screaming at them, so what was there? That doesn't mean that going to work magically clears that up, you know, you come home tired and you scream at them, too. But the important times are the times that you're really with them. It's the quality. And it's the quality of life. And it's the quality whether somebody is hooked up to a bunch of machines or if somebody is just enduring what they have from one day to the next and the next and the next. For whatever reasons, whether they're depressed or scared or because they don't know any better.

MOTHER: I think one of the coming ethical issues of our time . . . well, I was talking with [a medical geneticist] about this, about medical/ethical issues . . . and about abortion, and I said I'm glad I can cop out and say it's not my decision, and I'm not going to have any more children, so it's not an ethical decision I have to make. What I do think is a burning issue of our time is, When I no longer feel—and I don't mean out of an irrational depression—that I have a valid reason for continuing my life, do I have the right to end my life gracefully? If I am no longer productive to myself or society and that mere existence is all I have left, then I feel that's the time that I have the right to end my life. And I hope the medical and ethical help are there to help me do that if the time should come.

And I do feel this is true for me when you're talking about quality of life. I once said, having MS is, well, I'll never grow old. And I said I don't want to grow old. I don't want to be an old woman. Helpless and unproductive. And I thought, Well, I'll probably have a lot of other problems before I face that one! And so I do think this is an issue, a very heavy issue now.

COUNSELOR: There's no question. . . . And this has been one of my arguments with people in the psychology field, which I include myself, that some people are so insistent that the only reason for taking your life is irrational depression, and I think that is absolutely for the birds. Because I think that people can certainly take their own lives out of a feeling that now is the time that I choose to die. If they really are convinced that there is no way they can live again the kind of life that's bearable for them. And this varies with different people, because I have known some severely handicapped people who can lead quite adequate, from any standpoint, and to them obviously satisfactory kinds of lives.

MOTHER: I know people like that too. My favorite professor.

COUNSELOR: My father, who'd never been ill, and toward the end of his life became ill and died, very rapidly. And my feeling was just like yours with Meredith. Thank God! Because the minute he became incapacitated, he became a shell. It was like the light went out inside. And to me he died then. And this seems to happen to so many men in our society who have really accomplished things. Because we put the whole emphasis on what people accomplish and not what they are. Not on the being but on the doing. And my father was a doer.

MOTHER: I feel life to me is that way, too. Of course there are lots of adjustments to be made now that all of a sudden my whole life is turned upside down, but I have this great compulsion to do everything right now! Do everything, right now! And part of it's the freedom. I have a great deal of freedom now that Meredith is gone, freedom that I did not have and now I don't quite know what to do with it, so I'm trying to do everything. And again, a pressure to hurry up and decide what

I'm going to do so I'll get some order in my life and be secure, as if one is ever to really reach that point, but I've got to try. Putting my head in the sand doesn't accomplish anything, either. And I find that all very confusing. I want to live a full life until it's my time to go. I thought on the way down here, What if the plane crashes? Suits me. Because life has been very satisfying. I won't have missed anything.

IV

THE ISSUE
OF
SUDDEN DEATH

WE HAVE TALKED about terminally ill adults and children and the adjustment reactions these patients and their families pass through in an attempt to make some sense out of the happenings and to, perhaps, find some meaning or balance in the upset of their daily living. This is naturally only possible if there is time between the onset of an illness and the resulting death.

It is a fact, however, that thousands of adults and children die suddenly and unexpectedly. This means that the survivors are not prepared and often react with great shock and numbness to the tragic news at a time when clear thinking and fast actions are mandatory. The problems are manifold—and the following dialogue between an excellent and caring emergency-room nurse and the author will touch upon some of the issues and clarify again some questions most often asked.

When a patient is brought into the emergency room critically injured from an automobile accident, there is an air of great urgency and everyone is keenly aware that minutes count. Most hospital staffs unfortunately believe that there is neither the time nor the leisure to consider emotional needs. The victims must be screened quickly in order to decide which patient needs care most urgently, which ones can be helped, and whether or not the patient is really alive. Making this judgment is in itself an enormous task. The emergency-room physician must undertake to do whatever is necessary. Cardiac function must be maintained, airways must be cleared, oxygen started, IV fluids must be hung—all immediately. No one has the time to answer the desperate questions of the relatives inquiring after a husband or perhaps a little child. Emergency-room doctors and nurses are skillfully ministering to the physical demands of the dying patient; and furthest from their minds are the patient's psychological and spiritual needs at this time. They are frantically fighting to save a life. The critically ill or injured patient is often in a state of shock, both physically and emotionally, and he is usually not even aware of what is happening to him.

ML*: Dr. Ross, how can we help a patient who is conscious but is disoriented?

EKR: Yes, this happens often after a head injury. I think a nurse may be able to help this patient if she simply talks to him in a most brief and concrete manner, kind of orienting him. She can say, for example, "Mr. Jones, you have had an accident and you are in Bellemont Hospital. I'm Mrs. Smith and I'm trying to make you comfortable. Doctor Miller will be here shortly." This helps not only orienting him in terms of place, but it also tells him what happened to him and who you are.

ML: When critical patients are in the emergency room, one of our biggest concerns is the comfort of the relatives, but the nurses are so tied up and the relatives need them, but we can't help them.

EKR: Well, an especially trained volunteer or social worker, or the hospital chaplain, should be immediately available for the comfort of the relatives. These workers should be on call twenty-four hours a day; perhaps especially during the night hours, too, when the need may be greatest.

* ML is an emergency-room employee with years of experience and great compassion.

ML: Providing privacy for the relatives is a problem. We have conference rooms but not close to the emergency rooms.

EKR: I think in planning our new emergency rooms let's hope that provisions will be made for a special room for relatives. A room with an adequate space where families can ventilate their feelings, where they can sit in a comfortable chair; a room that will provide enough privacy so that it can be used for what they call a "screaming room."

ML: Sometimes we encounter unavoidable delays in reaching the coroner or the attending physician who will sign the death certificate or in reaching the surviving child who is legally the one we need to get in touch with.

EKR: We can't help these delays all the time, but no doubt they seem terribly needless and unkind to the family when you keep them waiting there without understanding really why we keep them waiting so long. I think this is where the volunteer comes in and where they can sit with them, listen to them, offer them soft drinks or coffee. This volunteer could offer to make some phone calls and help the relatives to talk. The relatives should not be left alone, except at their own request and only if they do not appear to be in too much emotional turmoil.

ML: Should we be on the lookout for any specific reaction from relatives that might be indicative of trouble?

EKR: I think a person who has just lost his only relative or who may feel responsible for an accident that caused the death is a very highly suicidal risk himself. He will often be in a state of shock and denial and he should not be allowed to leave the hospital alone.

ML: Well, what if there are no close friends to send this man home with, what would you suggest then?

EKR: If he is the driver of the car responsible for the death of the only relative he had and he is in a state of shock, I would admit such a relative to the hospital, and naturally not on a psychiatric unit, but a comfortable room, where he can receive warm and caring attention and adequate care at this time of emotional crisis. There may most likely be only one overnight stay anyway.

ML: Are you in favor of relatives such as this man and others being given a sedative to get them through this crisis period?

EKR: No, I think our tendencies very often to sedate the crying or screaming or hysterical relatives immediately . . . I wonder sometimes whether we do this to gratify our needs . . . you know, we would like to keep them quiet, we would like to prevent them from screaming, we wish that they would sign the papers fast and get out of the hospital. But I think we can help these people much better if we do not sedate them. Of course, if we do sedate them we will get them out of the emergency-room area fast. That doesn't really solve the problem for the relative, that only delays his reaction. And I think it would be better if they could cry and if they could ask questions and if they could sob on somebody's shoulder right there when it happened. I think you would do them a better service in the long run if you do not sedate them.

ML: The relatives who are very quiet and react little or not at all are the ones who worry me.

EKR: Well, they worry me, too. You should be very concerned about them. The people who cry and scream or act in what some people call a hysterical manner and are able to express their grief are much less of a risk than those who keep everything inside. We are talking now, of course, about sudden death; not the death that someone has been expecting, which may be a welcome relief from a long and debilitating illness.

ML: When there is a family accident with several people injured seriously, perhaps one has died, what should you say to the man who asks after his wife?

EKR: Well, I think if he himself is in a critical condition, perhaps needing surgical intervention, we need to wait to tell him that his wife is dead. The patient is already subjected to emotional trauma because of his injuries. He may go into shock or lose his will to live if we give him bad news immediately. There will be some exceptions to this, naturally. We had one very badly injured man whose wife was killed but his son was doing well. When the man asked about his family I said, "I'm not sure about your wife but I saw your son and he is doing well, and he asked about you." The man suddenly looked at me and said, "She's dead already, isn't she?" I nodded my head.

ML: It would have been very hard to lie to him at that point, wouldn't it have been?

EKR: Yes, I think if a man asks a straightforward question you have to tell him the truth. I then asked him if he could fight for his son's sake, and he said, "Yes, I will."

ML: Do you think patients who are conscious after an accident are really aware of what has happened to themselves and to others?

EKR: They are often in a state of shock. I think we must be very sensitive to each individual and decide how much a patient is able to hear. If we can be honest without shocking him and giving him unnecessary information which he's not asking for, I think we do the patient a great service.

ML: Sometimes a patient will ask if he is dying and he may be. . . . What would be the best answer to give him?

EKR: I think I've never told a patient that he is dying. The people who have done the poorest are the ones to whom information is given in a kind of a black-and-white fashion without any hope. It is very important that we allow for hope. I think in this situation you might simply say, "Boy, are we ever going to fight this out together." The patient is then going to trust you, that you do everything toward hope if you give him this kind of an answer. If he tells you, "Look, I know I'm going to die," I would then perhaps add, "It is possible but we can still try the best, can't we," so the patient knows that you are not going to lie to him but that you are sure trying to prevent this from happening.

ML: Recently during a resuscitation attempt a nurse in the group seemed to be having a very tough time after we had to give up. Her father had died a month or so before and she had returned to work only just recently.

EKR: You know, the members of the staff and their specific individual needs are terribly important. Nurses or physicians are going to be involved in many unsuccessful resuscitation attempts. These staff members bring into the picture their own special feelings, their own religious beliefs, perhaps their own unresolved griefs or bereavement so recent as to make the task much too painful. As soon as feasible it is important to take time to talk about the situation just past, so they can share and ventilate the feelings and that we can help them too, not just the patient and the family. They need a screaming room as badly as family members of accident victims!

ML: We usually do have a brief critique after a code blue or after a critical patient has been admitted to the hospital. But when we lose a patient, we feel so frustrated and often we are angry. It is very important that the staff can ventilate their feelings, too. I always say the staff needs a screaming room as much as anybody else. I can give you an example of how anger sounds sometimes and how difficult this is for the staff to take. Not too long ago we had three young people brought into the emergency room after a motorcycle accident. Two young men were dead on arrival, and one came in with a severed leg. He was mumbling, "It can't be, it can't be," and suddenly he started screaming, and then he was dead. The family heard him yell and tried to get into the room; it was a horrible sight and everybody tried to prevent the family from coming in. When they came to the door, they reacted with almost physical violence and started screaming, "What did you do to him, you killed him, you killed him." These kinds of bursts of anger and anguish and pain are terribly hard to take for the staff, who have their own feelings of anger, anguish, and frustration and many, many times they feel, Why did you die on me—and you know, they try so hard and then a patient dies on them. They have to be allowed to express these feelings, and that helps them tremendously.

ML: One night, after a long, unsuccessful fight to save a patient, a nurse overheard the family priest say to the relatives, "Well, it was God's will." The nurse blew up and stormed out of the department.

EKR: You know, when we are tired, we often misplace our anger, and nurses need to remember not to judge. I would be angry, too, if I would hear the priest say that. But, strange as it seems, many members of the clergy are very uncomfortable and frightened in the face of sudden and violent death, too. They haven't had time to prepare themselves for sudden tragedy and in attempting to console, they may grope for words and not find the right ones. Some ministers have little or no training along these lines at all. Nurses need to remember that it is the doctors' task to break the news to the family, and ministers who try to find the most comforting words are men with their own fears of death and . . . the unknown, and they are not as comfortable as we sometimes think they should be. The doctor or minister is a person with his own inability to cope with such things, the same as the rest of us, and that's sometimes hard to remember.

ML: Dr. Ross, how might the priest have handled this better?

EKR: Well, I think if the priest would have simply said, "If this would happen to me, maybe my consolation would be that this was God's will," then he would have allowed the family to say, "Well, this was not his relative," that's how those men talk. Or if it would have been a consolation, they would have borrowed his concept. "It's God's will" may imply "It is God's will so don't grieve and don't be angry." Most people would respond with tremendous resentment of God, and justifiably so! After such statements ministers have to learn how to accept the family's anger. Many of my patients have expressed fantastic anger at and questioning of God, and it is very hard for some members of the clergy to accept that. I have to give you an example of this:

I am seeing a woman now who had a marvelous, beautiful marriage, who had five little children. Her husband was an outdoors-type man and they decided they are not going to stay in the city, they are going to live in the country and have more time for the family and that clean, good, sound outdoor living. Her husband went to Colorado and called her up one day and said that he found a beautiful home, got a job, and that she should head west with the children in the car to join him. His last words to her were, "And then we will go skiing every day and we'll really start living." She packed her things, her parents went with the older children by car, and she stayed back for another day or two because one of the children had the flu. The next day she was informed by telephone that her husband was in an accident and he was killed instantly. When this woman came to me, she kept saying, "There is no God, there is no God, it is not possible." I listened to her and helped her ventilate her anguish and told her, "Next time when you come you are probably going to be very angry at God." She became angry at me and she said, "Didn't you hear, I said there is no God. He couldn't possibly do this!" The next time she came, she started to be very angry at God: "Why did He do this to me? Why did He deprive my children of a father?" She was very, very angry, and I pour fuel in the fire, I help them say those things. At the end of this session I told her that ultimately she may even find some meaning to this tragedy. She became increasingly angry with me, and I asked her to repeat once more what kind of a man her husband was, and her face lit up and she described him as an active sportsman, outgoing, always out-doors, and I just mentioned briefly, "Can you imagine what it would have been like if he had not been killed instantly? Maybe he would have been left paralyzed or unable to move or in a wheel chair?" She left without talking any further with me, and in the next session she came to me as if with a big revelation and she said, "You know, Dr. Ross, God must be a good God. Could you imagine what would have happened to my husband if he had not been killed but if he had stayed in a wheelchair, unable to move or talk to my children?" Do you see what I am trying to say? Families have to go through this anguish and rage, first denying God, then being angry at God, and then coming to grips and peace with God. So espe-cially if a member of the clergy is not judgmental but can even accept the patient's anger at God, or questioning of God, then he or she practices a true ministry of acceptance and uncon-ditional love.

ML: I can remember you saying it's all right to be angry with God because He's pretty big. He can take it.

EKR: I always say, when my chaplain students have trouble with that I say to them, "What's the matter with you? God can take it."

ML: Yes, I like that!

When we have tried unsuccessfully to revive a child or person, Dr. Ross, we find ourselves sometimes in a state of shock and denial. We feel unable to cope with the grieving parents, and we know that they need us but we are just so completely drained.

EKR: You see, I think sometimes it would be better if someone else who was not intimately involved in the recovery attempt could deal with the family. Just like a physician who has to do heart surgery on a child, it would be very hard for this man to take care of the emotional needs of this child and to kind of minister to his needs and answer his questions before surgery and then go ahead and do the surgery; it's very hard. That is why we need teams. If I can look after the emotional needs of this child and the surgeon can do his surgery it will really mean a good team. Then I think we can give what I call the ultimate, total patient care. The nurses and doctors who have just done their best and found that it wasn't good enough are not ready or able to help the waiting relative then. I think while the medical and nursing staff should attend the patient, another member of the team should be there for the next of kin—that can be a minister, a nurse, a social worker, or a grand volunteer, preferably a member of the Compassionate Friends. They should stay with the family as long as they want or need to stay in the hospital. It should be the physician, however, and not the nurse or the minister, who informs the family about the seriousness of the condition or about the fatal outcome. The reason for this is a simple one. If the physician is there to inform the family, the family concludes that he was also present when the patient was brought in. If no physician is in sight to give the next of kin the bad news, they very often assume that he was also not reachable when the accident victim was brought into the hospital. They will often wonder forever if the loved one might have been saved if help had been available fast.

We have seen a wife with a six-year-old child standing in a

hallway in one of our hospitals here in a state of shock when her husband was brought in apparently dead on arrival. A nurse, in what sounded like a cold and matter-of-fact manner, told his mother, in the hallway, "I guess you know that your husband is dead. Just sign these papers so we can remove the body!" Needless to say that the hurt and pain of this kind of a brutal confrontation will take a long time to heal. There is no excuse for giving such information in the public hallway or in front of small children who have not comprehended yet why they were suddenly rushed to a hospital, and it may result in a traumatic neurosis which is easily prevented if we could add a human touch to such a tragic moment.

ML: A doctor recently told me it takes all his energy to go out to the family that is totally unexpecting of bad news. Could someone perhaps prepare the family ahead of time that the situation is grave?

EKR: This would have to be done in a very skillful way, and the doctor should always be the one who actually tells the family even if it is hard; but you see in many cases there is not time to prepare the family. This is why I say that families, healthy families, should begin to come to grips with death and dying; talk to each other about what it would be like so that they can prepare themselves before such things happen.

ML: People react so differently to the news of their relatives' death.

EKR: Yes, and it's very hard to predict how anyone will react. Some people who are not in a stage of denial may berate the doctors and nurses and accuse them of not doing enough or of not doing the right thing. They may be angry with the ambulance driver or with each other. Sometimes we see husbands and wives fighting and arguing when their son was brought in dead, and it is very hard then, you know, to help these people who are in an almost irrational state of anger.

There again, I think if we do not judge them, but try to understand, that this is all an expression of their anguish and pain and grief.

ML: The emergency-room doctor has a grave responsibility when a call comes in, that a person is being brought in by the rescue team and is probably DOA [dead on arrival].

EKR: Yes, when a patient is in the hospital in CCU [cardiac care unit] and has a cardiac arrest, the nurses are quick to employ life-sustaining methods, electric shock, drugs, whatever is indicated; but the patient brought into the emergency room may not have adequate ventilation; he may not have had effective cardiac massage; indeed, he may have been dead before he was found. The house physician must then very quickly evaluate his patient. If there is any sign of life at all, if the patient has had good cardiac massage, if he has had adequate oxygen to his lungs, then this patient is a prime target for intensive resuscitation methods. There are tough moments when immediate decisions have to be made, and very often we attempt to revive a patient over too long a period. Sometimes it is because we want to use this as a learning experience, but I think we have to teach people more to think before we are doing this, and I think physicians have enough experiences so they don't have to use this on people where it's really hopeless.

I think if we could help people not only in the science of medicine but in the art of medicine—if we help staff to come to grips with their own hang-ups and their own fears of death, I think many of these desperate attempts would be prevented. Nurses and doctors should talk and share their feelings after such difficult cases. If you feel angry, say so; if you feel anguish and despair, say so; if you feel nothing at all, just emptiness, perhaps that is important to share, too. Nurses and physicians all need screaming rooms sometimes as much as the family does. If there weren't this peculiar hierarchy in medicine, where physicians feel that they ought not to share their feelings and where nurses are worried that they are not professional if they shed a tear, you know if we could get together sometimes simply as human beings and share grief and our anguish the working together would be much less strenuous.

ML: Do you think we should encourage relatives to see the body before they leave the hospital?

EKR: Yes, you see families that have been on a picnic, for example, and enjoyed a happy Sunday full of fun and sunshine and then suddenly, unbelievably, their little body drowns. Or a couple out of town on a shopping spree, Dad drops to the ground and immediately dies—perhaps from ruptured aneurysm. These are the families that will be in a state of profound shock and denial and will be just numb with grief and pain. These families should probably be encouraged to see and touch the body of their loved ones. They need very much to be in verbal and tactile communications with the deceased. Many people who have not been allowed or perhaps even didn't want to see the body have had troubles afterwards facing the reality of the same.

ML: Sometimes the body looks pretty grim, especially after a long attempt to resuscitate.

EKR: Well, I think the nurse should prepare the body by washing the face and hands with soap and water to remove emesis or blood or foul odor. You should leave the face uncovered if it is not too mutilated. If necessary, you have to elevate the head a few moments to clear up some of the sinuses. If there is a great damage done to the features, they should be covered by fresh linen and not newspaper, needless to say. The family should then be informed about the disfigurement, and the mutilated parts can be bandaged as for a postoperative patient. But I think you should aways give the family the option to see it anyway.

ML: Well, you sometimes feel anxious to get the relatives out and on their way, when you want to get the room cleaned up and send the body on to the morgue, and I suppose we are simply eager to be done with it.

EKR: Yes, this is tragic and this is our problem, and I think the first step to its improvement is to admit that a lot of things that we are doing, we are doing because of our own needs. You should never rush the relatives. You should allow time for dignity and privacy in this moment of really last togetherness. Before bringing in the family, you may want to move the body out of this cardiac room or major trauma room, into a small room which is less urgently needed, so that you do not have to rush the relatives to get out because another emergency might come in. And then all you have to do really is to put a chair or two nearby and allow them to be together without being rushed to get out of the room.

ML: It's difficult for me to ask relatives to make decisions— Do you want the wedding ring left on? Will you be taking the clothes with you? What funeral home should we call?

EKR: Of course! Most people have not been shopping for a funeral home during their lifetime. If the family is local, it is good if the ward secretary has already called the family's minister or priest or rabbi. If the family is Catholic, a priest should have been called immediately anyway. Those members of the helping professions expect to be called, day or night. And they can prove to be a fantastic aid to the nurses. If there is no church affiliation, the task may then fall to the friends to assist in the selection even of the funeral. As for religious medals or rings, I would leave them in place and wait to receive specific instructions from the family about them.

ML: Many times the family has just begun to regain composure after an outpouring of grief and anger only to be stirred up again; if in the case of an unexplained death, the coroner declares that it is a coroner's case and intends to do an autopsy.

EKR: This is difficult, but you know you have to tell the relative this. You have to tell them that they have no choice in the matter; but perhaps calling it an examination after death would make the procedure seem to be less brutal to them and explaining to the relatives that the physician performing this operation is a specialist with very specific diagnostic skills. Tell them that this disclosure from the study may turn up important information—perhaps for the surviving children— or it may help other patients in the future. Again, I think it depends a great deal whether you do this in a cold, detached manner or in a warm, understanding way, saying, "I know it is hard to talk about such things, but you know we just have to do it."

ML: We often wonder how families get on after the funeral and times later. Some of them seem destined for trouble, they were so devastated.

EKR: The people who have troubles and seem to have the most difficulties coming to grips with the problems, we found, are the ones who are suddenly and unexpectedly thrown into this situation—either by an accident, murder, or suicide—and those who cannot ever see the body—either because it is lost, as in a drowning, or destroyed in an explosion—or, I am remembering a family who lost somebody in a plane crash where there was no body. This is also true of families who have lost a son or a husband in Vietnam and no body has been returned. Those people often remain in a partial denial. They always feel maybe it was the wrong identification, and maybe it wasn't my son or my husband. Maybe he went over to the communists . . . a form of desperate hope that he is not dead. People who are allowed to see the body, who see any identifiable part of it, can face it better and can then begin to come to grips with it.

ML: We have the tendency to protect the family and discourage them from seeing the body when it is mutilated.

EKR: Yes, we do this especially often when there is a suicide or when people look very mutilated after accidents. But you have to understand that you are really not protecting the family; we do this for our own needs. You may be doing the family a great injustice. I think if you can clean up the body as carefully as possible—cover the most disfigured parts with clean linens—but don't deny the family that wish to be with the body or touch it or simply to view it. This will help them later on to face this grim reality.

ML: Do most families go through the stages of dying, moving from denial to anger, and then finally acceptance.

EKR: We found that people who are faced with sudden death, after this initial numbness and shock and denial, which very often lasts through the funeral where we are mechanically busy with a lot of things and a lot of relatives and visitors come—when all the relatives have gone, then this tremendous numbness sets in and the denial may last for weeks. We found that is also true of parents who have lost a child, who very often have to go through the stages of dying a second time after the death of the child. Many, many times afterwards, the mother stays home and remains in a stage of shock and denial, and the father, who can go out to work and switch gears and see other people and think other things, very often proceeds more quickly to the stage of anger. This is the reason why up to 75 percent of parents who have lost a child are on the verge of separation and divorce within the first year of the death of this child. What we could then do to these families is to help the ones who limp behind. That means in this case we should help the mother to express her anger so that the mother and father can get together through the anger, the bargaining, the depression, the ultimate acceptance. This is also true of families who have lost somebody suddenly. They will have to go through all these stages after death.

The emergency-room staff could greatly facilitate the grief resolution by calling these families approximately one month after the accident happened. It takes about that length of time for the family to get out of their stage of shock and denial. It is very important that the person who stayed with the relatives at the time of the tragedy—like the volunteer I mentioned earlier, or minister—that the same person calls the family about a month later and says, Would you like to come back to the emergency room and talk about it once more? Many families appreciate this greatly and then come back to the emergency room, into what I call the screaming room, and they sit with this volunteer or nurse or minister and they ask very, very understandable questions, like, Did he say anything? Did he open his eyes once more? Do you think he was conscious? Do you think he had a lot of pain? Did he know that he was dying? And you can talk with them about it and then only are they very often able to go through the stages. Then they can face the reality that, yes, it did happen and they are no longer alone in their anguish.

ML: Well, if we have them back for a conference like this, should we give them honest answers to the questions that they ask?

EKR: Well, I'm always in favor of honest answers, but it's not good to inflict more pain, so perhaps some things will have to go unanswered. If the members of the helping profession can answer some of these questions in a reassuring way, it will help the family a great deal to proceed alone from denial to acceptance. I guess, in summary, we see that the emergency-

room nurse and the physician have more special jobs to perform. This is also true of the specially trained volunteer or
the clergy. There are physicians and nurses who take care of
the patients and who have to remain outwardly calm during
this crisis, often concealing their own anxieties and emotions.
They must quickly and with expertise perform exacting and
lifesaving techniques, and they must control their own distress, very often their own anger, when that effort to save a
life sometimes fails. Sudden death, ultimately when the victim
is a virile-looking young man or a young woman, shocking
when it is suicide, overwhelming when it is a child, outraged
when caused by carelessness or intention—these are all feelings the emergency-room staff must share and work through
so that each one can be most effective in reacting with the
family and can facilitate the grief process in the first few
hours and moments after death. It is my hope that more
emergency rooms will provide a screaming room for the families and for the staff to use later on; and that they call the
families once in a while later on to see if they have unfinished
business or questions that they might answer. It is hoped that
the emergency-room staff members will learn also to come to
grips with the idea of their own death—without fear—and
will then be able to communicate much better this inner calm
to others.

In my five-day live-in retreat workshops as well as in our
Shanti Nilaya Growth and Healing Center, thousands of health
professionals and lay people come to seek help with their fears
and bottled-up emotions.

It is an opportunity for them to drop their masks of efficiency
and professionalism, of the stoical front and avoidance of painful memories. In a safe environment, assisted by a highly trained
staff, they are able to relive traumatic experiences, face old

fears, guilt, and shame, and emerge with a sense of greater empathy and inner freedom.

Unless every hospital and clinic, every business office and household, has a safe room where emerging negative and painful emotions can be openly expressed, we will never have enough facilities (counseling centers and growth and healing retreat centers) to gratify all the needs of our population.

If we could externalize our own fears and share our own unfinished business, we would not have to resort to prescribing Valium—which really does not sedate the survivor but sedates, unfortunately, our own conscience.